TESTIMONIALS A
ENDORSEMENTS

'Clare is an exceptionally well informed adviser on all things retail. In this fast-moving, fast-changing industry what she doesn't know isn't worth knowing. She has worked with, and shared her wide retail experience with, everyone from Chief Executives of large national chains to independent start-ups, niche suppliers, and individuals looking for a new career direction. This much-anticipated book fills a gap that will give real, practical knowledge to help anyone trying to make their mark as a supplier to retail.' **Patrick Ballin, Former Head of Global Supply Chain and Logistics Development at The Body Shop**

'Clare Rayner is like a stick of rock, cut her in half and you would find the word "retail" running right through her. It's in her blood. Not only has she spent all her life at the coal face of retail, she has the technical knowledge to back it up. Forget broad brush approaches, Clare gets down to detail and answers all the questions, stupid and otherwise, that you've ever wanted to ask about growing your business. Her punchy no-nonsense style is for everyone involved in the business of supplying customers with what they want. You can't get a better, more supportive handbook for success.' **Penny Haslam, TV Business Presenter (as seen on** *Breakfast***, BBC News)**

'Clare is the real deal. With The Retail Champion on your side you get straight talking, no-nonsense advice. If you want to grow your business by selling to retailers then you will ignore this book at your peril!' **Bill Morrow, Founder of Angels Den, a Global Network of Business Investment Angels**

'Clare's enthusiastic approach and practical expertise will offer brands who want to sell to retailers invaluable insight to getting their product to market. It can be daunting approaching retailers to pitch your product (or service); this book is the perfect "cheat sheet" to get you started!' **Kerry Bannigan, CEO & Co-Founder of Nolcha Fashion Week, New York. Global Founder of Independent Retailer Month**

'Think BIG – Clare's wealth of experience both as a Retailer and as a Service Provider to retailers provides fantastic insight into the art of relationship selling to the Retail Sector. In this book Clare delivers incredible insights into the world of modern retail, what a retail buyer looks for in their suppliers, and navigates the pitfalls and opportunities when negotiating with a retailer. A fantastic read from cover to cover.' **Scott Storey, Managing Director of EPOS Partners**

'Clare's personal experience of the retail industry and wealth of expertise in dealing with companies of all sizes give her a unique insight into how retailer–supplier relationships work. Anyone wanting to sell their products or services to a retailer would be mad not to read this first...' **Helen Goworek, Senior Lecturer in Marketing, Nottingham Trent University, author of *Fashion Buying***

'Why wasn't this book available when we needed it three years ago!? Insider knowledge of how retailers operate is crucial. Retailers are very different to the corporate IT world we came from; Clare's guidance in our 1-2-1 mentoring sessions was invaluable to Garmentology. On behalf of everyone who is going to read your book, and benefit from you sharing your knowledge, Thank you Clare!' **Susanne Newman, Founder of Garmentology (service provider to retailers)**

'The team at Being U had no retail experience when we went to Clare. We had grand ideas, we knew a lot about our market, we thought we had all the focus we needed. All that changed after my first meeting with Clare. It became apparent that without Clare's input we might have failed. Over the period we worked together we discovered that Clare is actually ALWAYS right! So if you want to sell to retailers you must do one thing – get her book. If you follow Clare's advice your chances of success will dramatically increase!' **Sadia Sisay, Founder of Being U (product supplier to retailers)**

'*How to Sell to Retailers* is an excellent guide for any small business who wants to compete in a competitive marketplace. It's easy to assume that you are "too small" to fight for business with major retailers, but, in this comprehensive guide, Clare Rayner offers common sense and easy to implement advice that will enable businesses of any size to build the client list they dream of.

'I'm delighted to see that networking, social networking sites such as LinkedIn, and asking for referrals are covered. Many business development books overlook these vital areas of marketing or take them for granted.' **Andy Lopata, author of *...And Death Came Third!: The Definitive Guide to Networking and Speaking in Public* and *Recommended: How to Sell Through Networking and Referrals***

How to Sell to Retail

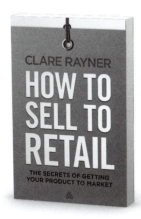

How to Sell to Retail

The secrets of getting your product to market

Clare Rayner

KoganPage

LONDON PHILADELPHIA NEW DELHI

First published in Great Britain and the United States in 2013 by Kogan Page Limited

120 Pentonville Road	1518 Walnut Street, Suite 1100	4737/23 Ansari Road
London N1 9JN	Philadelphia PA 19102	Daryaganj
United Kingdom	USA	New Delhi 110002
www.koganpage.com		India

© Clare Rayner, 2013

The right of Clare Rayner to be identified as the author of this work has been asserted by her in accordance with the Copyright, Designs and Patents Act 1988.

ISBN   978 0 7494 6680 0
E-ISBN   978 0 7494 6681 7

British Library Cataloguing-in-Publication Data

A CIP record for this book is available from the British Library.

Library of Congress Cataloging-in-Publication Data

Rayner, Clare.
     How to sell to retail : the secrets of getting your product to market / Clare Rayner.
          p. cm.
     ISBN 978-0-7494-6680-0 (pbk.) – ISBN 978-0-7494-6681-7 (ebook)   1. Retail trade.
2. Marketing.   I.   Title.
     HF5429.R3448 2013
     658.8'04–dc23
                                                                                         2012039396

Typeset by Graphicraft Limited, Hong Kong
Printed and bound in India by Replika Press Pvt Ltd

*Thanks to all those who have supported me
in writing this book – you know who you are!*

CONTENTS

PART FOUR Get Big, Stay Big! 189

FOREWORD

I was first introduced to Clare Rayner by a mutual connection in 2009. Clare invited me to speak at a new event she was organizing for the benefit of entrepreneurs and SMEs (small and medium-sized enterprises) in Hertfordshire, where she was based. The purpose of the event was to engage and inspire a broad range of local business owners, to give them some great advice and motivation that would help them to recharge their batteries, and to enable them to go back to work with renewed vigour and enthusiasm in spite of the testing marketing conditions and recessionary economy.

Since that first meeting I've been struck by how enterprising Clare is, and how passionate she is about inspiring entrepreneurs. Having had a 1-2-1 with her I realized that I've never met anyone who is quite so knowledgeable about retailers and retailing; and I've met a lot of entrepreneurs as you can imagine!

The foreword to her first book, *The Retail Champion: 10 Steps to Retail Success*, was written by Mike Clare – an inspirational retail entrepreneur himself and someone I greatly admire for his business acumen. I was delighted to be invited to offer the foreword to this book, as what Clare has set out to achieve is very relevant to a wide range of business people – some who might not even have started their businesses yet; some who need just this advice to help them really accelerate their growth and launch their product (or service) to the market through the major national and international retail chains.

This book epitomizes how much Clare has to share and how eager she is to give her knowledge for the benefit of other business owners. *How to Sell to Retail* is a comprehensive guide that should enable those who have an idea for a product or business solution to success-fully sell to retailers. As Clare says, it is extremely difficult for a small, unknown brand to break into the market and to begin to sell their products or services to a retail giant. However, the four logical sections, broken down into 12 clear parts, provide a structured approach that walks the reader through each of the necessary ingredients that will help them succeed. Interestingly, much of the approach that Clare takes is equally relevant for any business that wants to present their idea to investors too! With each section leading into the next, the outcome is a powerful and prioritized action plan that gives business owners real clarity about where to focus their efforts in order to take their businesses to the next level.

Clare's style is conversational, supportive and open – this book is easy to read and enjoyable, full of case studies that really bring the points to life, and it is supported with free downloadable resources. The approach can be used time and time again, providing a business owner with a structure that will enable them to review, refresh and further develop their own unique action plan.

The focus on helping a business owner to develop 'robust and repeatable processes and systems in order to create a scalable, sale-able enterprise' is exactly what I look for when assessing a business for its investment potential. So, whether you are an established brand or just thinking of starting up, my advice is to take time to work through this book – you will undoubtedly benefit from it!

I wish you success, and, as I say in my talks: 'Start small, think big, move fast'.

Julie Meyer MBE, one of BBC's Online Dragons. Founder and CEO of Ariadne Capital, Founder of Entrepreneur Country, Managing Partner of Ariadne Capital Entrepreneurs Fund [ACE]

BIOGRAPHY

Clare Rayner, The Retail Champion, is one of the most well-known and respected retail experts in the United Kingdom, championing for the success and sustainability of smaller, independent retailers and suppliers to retail. A child born into a family of retailers and entrepreneurs, she is passionate about retail and business: it is in her blood.

Clare started out as a fast-track graduate store management trainee for McDonald's and went on to work with leading retailers such as M&S, Dixons and Argos. She moved swiftly into management roles before being headhunted into senior consulting roles with global software giant SAP, and international management consulting brand Accenture. Clare is engaged by clients as a retail consultant, retail speaker and retail mentor. In 2011 she was invited to launch Independent Retailer Month in the UK, a global 'Shop Local' campaign which runs throughout July. She is founder and host of 'The Retail Conference', a highly respected annual retail industry event.

Clare is a frequent media contributor, regularly featured on BBC TV News, various radio broadcasts, within trade press and digital media, commenting on a wide range of retail and consumer topics. Clare owns a number of brands that service the retail sector. These include:

- The Retail Champion
- The Retail Conference
- Retail Acumen
- e-mphasis Internet Marketing

More details about each of these brands are included in the appendices.

RESOURCES

How to Sell to Retail is packed full of practical resources and templates, so you can put learning into practice immediately. These are also available online exclusively for readers – you'll find out how you can download them on page 6. Your reader code is: **123213**.

Introduction

This book has been written for *you*: business owners, start-ups, pre-start-ups and *anyone* with a *big* idea who wants to develop and sell products or services to the big retail chains.

If you are a garage inventor, bedroom-based business or dining table designer, this book is for you! If you dream of becoming the founder of the next Innocent Smoothies, the next James Dyson, this book can help you with a step-by-step, structured approach. We will walk through a 12-point plan, broken down into four sections, so that you can learn how to look big, plan big, pitch big, get big and stay big through successfully selling to retailers.

With a practical focus, and including examples, case studies, checklists and action plans, I've written this book to help you make your big idea a reality. By reading this book and completing the actions on your checklists you will learn the key ingredients that you should have in place in order to make it *big* and you will be able to implement what you need to succeed.

My inspiration

Since 2010 at least half of my 1-2-1 mentoring clients at any given time have been new start-ups, even pre-start-ups, who wanted to get a better idea about how to sell to retailers. They came to me for a critique of their idea, of their pitch, or for support with their go-to-market strategy. They also came to me to see if I could help them get a 'foot in the door', having seen on tools such as LinkedIn that my network includes some very senior decision makers at retailers that they'd love to have as customers.

Many of those who approached me were not yet generating revenue and had little enough money to launch the business, let alone pay for my professional services. I gave as much assistance as I could, pointed them at my blog etc, but it was never going to be the same as working together 1-2-1.

It seemed that there were many people with a *big* idea who simply didn't know how to take it further. Many people told me they felt trapped in their day job, spending every moment of their free time designing and developing ideas, not knowing where to go next. I wanted to provide anyone who felt that way with a robust framework that would give them the confidence to jump off their current treadmill (when the time was right) and make a break for the freedom of entrepreneurialism. It seemed that so many people didn't know how or when to make the jump and were quite rightly scared of the impacts and risks of walking away from a 'secure job' to start out on their own. Obviously it is a balance, and for people with family and financial commitments only they can know when the time is right, *but* by sharing the 12-point plan my hope is that more of those ideas will make it out of the bedrooms, garages, sheds and brains of the creative people behind them and make it to market.

Having been through the process of writing my first book, *The Retail Champion: 10 Steps to Retail Success*, I realized that I could give more substantial help to those who would benefit from it (albeit not the same as working together 1-2-1) if I captured my approach for 'suppliers to retail' in a second book. And so it began! I returned to Kogan Page with the outline idea and obviously it came to fruition. '*How to Sell to Retail: The secrets of getting your product to market*' is the result; I hope you enjoy it.

My background

Nowadays I am known as The Retail Champion and I am engaged by clients as a mentor, consultant and professional speaker. I am often invited by BBC TV, radio and trade press to comment on retail matters.

Through my main business, which I co-founded with my husband, Andrew, I own and run five brands:

- The Retail Champion: 1-2-1 mentoring for retailers and suppliers to retail;
- Independent Retailer Month UK: the UK arm of a global, shop local, campaign;
- The Retail Conference: the UK's leading annual retail industry event;
- Retail Acumen: consulting and analytics for larger retailers and consumer brands;
- e-mphasis Internet Marketing: a digital marketing agency with a specific focus on local search marketing.

If that wasn't enough, we turned the surplus space in our own offices into a serviced and virtual office solution for local, small businesses (Albans Office Space) *and* because of my husband's love of technology he's been retailing clearance business technology items since 2007 as well! You can find out more about my business interests in the appendices.

Of course, I have had a long career path over many years that enabled me to get to this position: running a number of successful small businesses, writing this book, and sharing my learnings and experiences from that career with you. However, my learning didn't start with my career. I was a child born into a family of entrepreneurs, with a retail bias dating back over 150 years. I don't recall ever *not* being involved with or surrounded by retailers, manufacturers, importers or wholesalers – so I picked up a huge amount of know-how, without realizing it at the time, just from the family contacts!

My parents ran a successful fine-furnishings business, which they sold in the 1990s to retire. For over 20 years they operated what would today be described as a multi-channel retail brand, although they pre-dated the internet! They had several retail outlets, concessions in other stores (they sold through a couple of major chains), a mail order catalogue and a factory shop. Rather than buying in goods to resell, their model was to make to order, a bespoke service for each customer uniquely, so they additionally had full warehousing and manufacturing capabilities.

My grandparents also had a factory and a shop, selling home furnishing products to the regional Co-op chain. My uncle ran an abattoir and butchery, supplying meat products to a wide range of local retailers and smaller grocery chains. My great grandfather had been an importer and wholesaler of fruit and vegetables, as had his father before him, selling fresh produce from Old Covent Garden market to retailers, restaurants and other markets – and so it continues, as far up the family tree as I have attempted to trace.

I was always interested in business, making money, having ideas and implementing them. As a teenager I had a myriad of jobs, although not always for the family business (it just isn't that cool to work for your parents!). In the school holidays I juggled working in a service station with an attached convenience store, working in my parents' showroom, covering the reception in a beauty salon *and* being a quality control laboratory assistant in the local photographic studio! If that wasn't enough, I used to collect remnants of fabric at my parents' factory, and stray elastic bands from the bundles of postal enquiries that arrived each day, to make them up into funky 'scrunchies' (hair bands) using the sewing machines in the factory out of hours. I retailed these to fellow schoolmates for £1 an item.

When tired of my hair-band empire I began to organize outings to theme parks such as Alton Towers. I'd book the coach and negotiate a group ticket price. I'd work out a price point for the trip as a package that would be acceptable to my school friends based on known pocket-money rates. I'd calculate how many tickets I needed to sell to break even (to cover the fixed cost of the coach and the entry price to the park), so from that I'd know what the margin per additional sale was, thus how much money I was making on the event overall.

Yes, that entrepreneurial streak that had been in my family for over a century was part of my fabric too!

I didn't immediately decide to launch my own business and follow in my family's entrepreneurial footsteps; I was attracted to the 'bright lights and big city', so moved to London. I'd spent my teenage years in the countryside long before such things as mobile phones and the internet, so I was keen to see some 'life'. Breaking the family mould I tried my hand at academia and took up a place on a four-year

MEng in Chemical Engineering at Imperial College in London. I'd got all the ingredients to be a first-class honours student – bar one: the desire to be on a production-line education system for the next four years... My calling was to be out there earning money. I dropped out of university and started working. By day I was managing a luxury shoe concession in Harvey Nichols, by night I was a crew member in my local McDonald's. At about the same time I bought my first property; I was 19. In keeping with that entrepreneurial streak I rented out the spare rooms so that the rental income covered the mortgage. Being 19, that meant that I was able to enjoy spending my salary and had a lot of fun!

I guess it was a number of things that made my regional manager take notice of me – such as advertising for flatmates in the staff room, or turning up to work at McDonald's in a very smart outfit (from Harvey Nichols) and doing a quick change into my uniform. He put me on their graduate training programme – and to this day, hand on heart, it was the best 'how to run a business' course I can say I've ever had. McDonald's really empower their management – but within a clearly laid down framework. The secret to their success is their ability to offer consistency in both service and product quality in any store around the world. It was my experience at McDonald's that cemented my belief that if a business wants to become a successful, scalable, saleable enterprise they first need to have robust, repeatable processes and systems. That's stayed with me ever since!

From McDonald's I went on to work in buying and merchandising roles with retailers including Marks and Spencer, Safeway (now Morrison's), BHS, Dixons and Argos. During my time at Argos I was headhunted by global software giant SAP and joined their retail go-to-market team. This was my first opportunity to sit on the supplier side of the table in the sales process – until that point I'd always been the buyer. After SAP I worked for a period of time at Accenture, the management consulting brand, before deciding the time was right to stop being someone's employee and to finally follow in the family footsteps and start out on my own. You can read all about my past career on LinkedIn via **www.linkedin.com/in/clarerayner**.

So what is the 12-point plan?

It is notoriously difficult for a small, unknown brand to sell products or services to a retail giant. Feared for their ruthless buying habits, fierce negotiation skills and the ability to swiftly reproduce *your* ideas, pitching to a retailer can be a double-edged sword.

The 12-point plan has been proven to help smaller businesses to sell successfully to retailers. It includes the critical ingredients that will not only make retail buyers sit up and listen, but will help you establish a quality, long-term relationship with a retail organization.

Working through the 12-point plan, you will learn how to look big, plan big, pitch big, get big and stay big:

1 *Look Big*: this part includes your business identity, your business presence and your people.

2 *Plan Big*: focusing on your competition, your ideal customer and your scalability.

3 *Pitch Big*: delving into the details of preparation, the process of selling and the often-feared negotiation.

4 *Get Big, Stay Big*: finally considering your plans for expansion, underpinning your growth with replication and maintaining a healthy dose of paranoia!

In the main text there are several checklists that you can complete. If you would rather not write directly on the book, you can access my exclusive client-only download area which I've made available to all readers of this book via **www.retailchampion.co.uk/selling-to-retailers/resources**. Here you will find all the checklists, templates and tools referenced throughout this book available for download. To access this area for the first time you need to request a 'pin' – you do so by filling in the request form on the right of the webpage, including the special reader code on page xvi of this book. A pin will then be e-mailed out to you that you can use to log in via the main prompt on the webpage.

It's important to work through each element of the 12-point plan sequentially, as each lays down the foundations for the next. The whole builds up into a robust platform for your business not only to sell successfully to retailers, but to grow and mature. It may look relatively easy on the surface, but if it were, you'd have done it before! The devil is in the detail, and you can't cut corners because you'll come unstuck. We want your business to be a robust, reliable and professional supplier to retail and we can't achieve that if it's 'a house of cards'. Do work through each section; some will need more focus, others will just need a quick check to validate that all is well.

Good luck in your journey. I know it will be an exciting one and I wish you every success!

PART ONE
Look Big

As I said in the Introduction, retailers are cautious about who they do business with. It's natural that big companies feel safer buying from other big companies; they believe that with size comes security – financial security and a proven track record of delivering on customer promises. They believe that buying from a big company reduces risk, risk that they would associate with buying from a smaller, less financially robust company, with little or no proven track record. Retailers are not generally big risk takers, so much of the focus of this part of the book is on how to mitigate those risks that big companies consider to be inherent in smaller businesses.

Throughout Part One we'll be making sure that when you present your business to a retail buyer they will have no reason to doubt your calibre, credibility or capability just because of your size. In fact we want to make your proposition so compelling to the buyer that the question of size doesn't even enter their head. The fundamental reason for all of this is to ensure that you can punch above your weight, that you look big, look credible and at least as low risk as big business would be perceived to be. There is a saying 'dress for the job you want, not the job you've got' – essentially this is the same sentiment, except its application is to your whole business and not just to an individual (although the individuals who represent your business should also present themselves well!).

While we could get drawn into a debate about how shallow our society is to be swayed by appearances, and how in fact we should judge things on merit, it's a simple fact of human nature that judgements *are* formed, and almost instantly, based on appearances, rightly or wrongly. As canny business people, eager for success, we need to operate most effectively within the social structure that exists. As this is unlikely to change for the foreseeable future, as business owners we need to put our best foot forward and focus on looking big.

Through the three chapters in this part of the book we'll explore your:

1 business identity;

2 business presence;

3 people.

At the end of this part we'll do a recap on the key components of 'looking big', with a checklist for you to go through to make sure you've got all the necessary ingredients in place.

Identity

Introduction

As promised, this chapter will focus on the identity of your business. We will be focusing on how to:

- articulate exactly what your business is about by creating a mission statement;

- use your mission statement to really engage your team, suppliers, customers and wider stakeholder network and to validate decisions;

- leverage the 'softer' aspects of the business's 'personality' and culture to demonstrate to potential clients that you have the right approach and attitude towards the sensitive issues of ethics, environment and sourcing;

- define your positioning, and understand the effect that positioning can have on the expectations of those who deal with you.

Once we've laid down these foundations we'll focus in more detail on the important role of the 'presentation' aspect of the positioning piece by looking at your visual identity and brand image in detail. We'll consider:

- the importance of having the right presentation;

- how 'brand' is a key contributor to the ability to 'punch above your weight';

- why all outward representation of your brand, both physical materials and also online content, can make a difference to how you are perceived.

What is a mission statement?

A mission statement is a clear and concise message that encapsulates the business purpose into about 50 words. It really only takes about 20 minutes to write and finesse (when you focus on it), and when you've 'got it' you'll feel proud, certain – you'll think 'yes, that *is* what my business is about'. It's a great way for you to communicate the guiding principles of your business to others – suppliers, customers, staff, anyone – in order to get them to understand, in a nutshell, what it is that the business does. I've also found it's a fantastic tool to use at those group events where you have to stand up and tell a room full of strangers who you are and what you do. Instead of going blank, or waffling, you can state: 'My name is [Joe Bloggs] and I represent/own/ am launching [company name]. At company name we [add mission].' And that's it!

However, your mission is far more useful than being just a tool that stops you from going blank when networking. We'll look at the ways you can use it in Part Two. Right now, let's look at how to create yours.

How to create your mission statement

In order to create your mission statement you first need to understand what it comprises. Typically a good mission statement should be about 50–60 words and it should include four key components:

1 **Proposition**: what you offer. You should explain, as clearly as possible (so that anyone can understand it), what your business sells (products and/or services).

2 **Target market**: who you offer it to. Define who you (ideally) sell to; this is a generic description of your customer group.

3 **Delivery**: what your service proposition is. Outline how you deliver your offer to the customer and what is, or is not,

included in the process. Just to clarify, I do not mean 'deliver' in the context of physical logistics – I mean fulfilling the customer promise.

4 **Outcome**: what the outcome is for your customer. Describe how your customer should benefit from buying from you, what the experience of buying from you achieves for them.

Example mission statements

In order to bring this concept to life I'm going to share the mission statements for two very different businesses that I own: The Retail Champion and Albans Office Space.

1. The Retail Champion mission

'The Retail Champion offers retail expertise and bespoke business mentoring programmes to business owners who are either retailers or suppliers to retail. With The Retail Champion businesses will develop robust and repeatable processes and systems, underpinning their future growth and success. The Retail Champion programmes help businesses to become scalable, saleable enterprises.' (52 words)

When you start to create your mission statement my advice would be to begin by writing a statement to answer each of the constituent parts, then knit it together, finessing the wording once you're happy with each element. Looking again at the statement for The Retail Champion, this was built up from:

1 **Proposition**: what you offer. 'The Retail Champion offers retail expertise and bespoke mentoring programmes...'

2 **Target market**: who you offer it to. '...to business owners who are either retailers or suppliers to retail.'

3 **Delivery**: what your service proposition is. 'With The Retail Champion businesses will develop robust and repeatable processes and systems, underpinning their future growth and success.'

4 **Outcome**: what the outcome is for your customer. 'The Retail Champion programmes help businesses to become scalable, saleable enterprises.'

I'm sure I could polish and finesse it further, but frankly I stopped myself spending hours on it once I felt satisfied that it said enough about what I offer, to whom, how I deliver, and what my customers' experiences are as a result. I was happy to share and publish that statement and I felt confident that it *did* match what I offered. When doing yours, remember to do the same; you don't have to spend hours on it, just get to a place where it feels 'good' (not necessarily perfect) and then stop. You can always come back to it at a later date if you feel it's not quite representative of the business.

2. Albans Office Space

I also own another business, completely separately from my retail-centric brands. This is a serviced and virtual office based in St Albans, rather appropriately called 'Albans Office Space'. This is a very different proposition from The Retail Champion. I'm going to share the mission statement for Albans Office Space as it will help to illustrate that irrespective of what you offer, or who you offer it to, your mission statement is very powerful. It will not be a waste of your time to spend 20–30 minutes or so working it out.

'Albans Office Space offers flexible workspace, meeting facilities and virtual office services to business people who want to work at, meet in or grow their business from our St Albans location. We are friendly, welcoming and supportive of customer needs so customers feel that their business is as important to us as our own.' (54 words)

1 **The proposition**: what you offer. 'Albans Office Space offers flexible workspace, meeting facilities and virtual office services...'

2 **The target market**: who you offer it to. '...to business people who want to work at, meet in or grow their business from our St Albans location.'

3 **The delivery**: your service proposition. 'We are friendly, welcoming and supportive of customer needs...'

4 **The outcome for your customer**: '...so customers feel that their business is as important to us as our own.'

As you can probably see from the above, the mission statement really helps 'ground' the business and encapsulates all that it stands for in a way that is readily understandable to anyone else. It very clearly states who the service is ideally offered to and what it feels like to be a customer.

As a supplier to retail, particularly if you are supplying products for resale as opposed to services, it may be worth considering defining two mission statements for your business. One can focus on the end user of your product while the other can focus on your buyer, so that you can build a really clear picture of what your business presents to both of your customer groups. When working with clients who are suppliers of product to retailers, I've found that creating both really helps them focus on their approach and value proposition by clearly defining who they are ultimately selling to (the consumer) and who they are selling through (the retailers). So while it takes a little extra time to create both, it really will help later when you are thinking in more detail about the value proposition and go-to-market strategy. With two versions of your mission statement you can ensure that you've focused adequately both on your retail channel to the consumer and on the consumers themselves. By having two versions, and basing your business operations on ensuring that you live up to them, you should be more aware of how to deliver a business proposition that ensures both groups are satisfied with the outcome.

How to use your mission statement

As I mentioned above, you can use your completed mission statement in a variety of ways. It can provide you with a succinct 'elevator pitch' when you're asked the dreaded question 'what do you do?' and is an effective way to communicate the essence of the business when you bring in new staff.

I use the mission statements for each of my brands to introduce new staff to what each of the different business areas do. I also use it on the 'about' page of my website and on marketing materials. Some people will feel attracted to what I say in my mission statement whereas others will not; of course, it's designed to appeal to, and resonate with, the ideal customer. Using it in 'first contact' enables a natural filtering process to take place – potential employees, customers and suppliers will think 'that's the kind of business I want to work for/with', and those who aren't a good fit may just think 'that doesn't sound right for me' and will probably not make contact. It saves everyone time in that respect!

Think about how you could use a mission statement. As you grow your business and need to engage staff/suppliers/outsourcing partners, could you use your mission statement as part of an introduction to your business? Could you use each element, expanded into more detail, to really give them an overview of your business and your vision? It would be a useful way to get your 'team' (internal and third parties) all working together for a common aim. I've found that my staff engagement levels increase when I talk them through the mission statements for each of my businesses. If I take time to explain, to break it down, and stick to the basic four elements, I can see that they really begin to understand what each business area/brand is all about and therefore are more productive as their efforts are focused on achieving the mission.

You can also use the mission statement to sense-check decisions. In the case of Albans Office Space I'm not generally active in the day-to-day running of that business, so for me, as one of the owning directors, I find that the mission statement can act as a 'conscience' for the business. When the team seek advice on a decision or issue, rather than appear to be making decisions for them, I can ask something like 'what would be the best thing to do in order to meet our mission?' Then we're working together, looking at possible solutions that are best for the mission. Equally, if the team want to invest in making some changes they can present their idea to me. If they can demonstrate that the proposal is supportive of the mission (and that it has reasonable payback, of course) then I'll be much more likely to sign it off. If they can't explain what benefit the action has in the context of the mission I will ask them to reconsider their plans.

This approach, using the mission statement in team decision making, removes the risk of it becoming personal. Rather than the team grumbling that their proposal has been turned down because 'the boss just didn't like my idea', the emotion is removed and the team member will more likely be thinking 'how can this idea be made better so that it fits with the business mission?' – they'll still be disappointed not to have had approval *but* they won't feel it's a decision based on emotions, they'll understand it's based on what's best for the business. A far easier pill to swallow! As your business grows you may need to use your mission statement in this way, even to check that your own ideas are valid, and this approach will mean that your mission statement will become of great value to you, especially as you grow and need to have others taking delegated decisions for you that are all still in the best interest of your business.

Finally, worthy of mention is that although your mission is the key message that explains what your business is about to all those involved, it should not constrain your business. As you grow you also need to evolve, and there could be a time when you need to undertake a strategic review of what your business, in totality, is all about. If you determine that your future success is dependent on a change in direction or focus, you will need to update your mission statement. At that point, of course, it can be used as a positive message to all your stakeholders – staff, customers, suppliers etc – to communicate the change, the reasons and the exciting new direction.

Of course, that is likely to be a while away, but it's important to note that your mission isn't cast in stone but that it is a key foundation for the business and it should only be changed when there is good reason.

So, it's over to you at this point. Before we move on I'd like you to take some time out, while it's all fresh in your mind, and focus on creating your mission statement in the grids shown in Figures 1.1 and 1.2. When you've got a few words for each element you need to knit them together to create a 50–60-word mission statement that you feel proud of.

As already mentioned, if you would rather not write directly on the book, you can access my exclusive client-only download area which I've made available to all readers of this book. Here you will find the grids, as well as various other templates and tools referenced throughout this book, available for download. To access this area for the first time you need to request a 'pin' – you do so by filling in the request form on the right-hand side of the webpage, including the special reader code from the inside front cover of the book. A pin will then be e-mailed to you that you can use to log in via the main prompt on the page. To see the download area visit **www.retailchampion.co.uk/ selling-to-retailers/resources.**

Complete Figure 1.1 to determine what your mission is when you focus on your end user.

FIGURE 1.1   Defining the mission statement for your *end user*

Mission statement element	YOUR answer (end-user focused)
Your proposition	
Your target market	
Your service delivery	
The outcome for your customer	

Complete Figure 1.2 to determine what your mission is when you focus on your buyer.

FIGURE 1.2   Defining the mission statement for your *buyer*

Mission statement element	YOUR answer (retail-buyer focused)
Your proposition	
Your target market	
Your service delivery	
The outcome for your customer	

Now you've got clarity on your mission, we're going to consider your culture and values – which are also foundations of your business.

Culture, values and ethics

The business culture, values and ethics you bring to the business define its unique personality and are key factors which will come up later when you're pitching to retailers. As a business owner it's important to be mindful of the 'boundaries' or 'rules' you want to have for your business as this will help clarify what is acceptable for the business and what are 'no-go areas'. This clarity is essential when you start to work with others – staff, suppliers and third parties – so that they understand the business ethos and can work with you to achieve it. As with the mission, your culture and values will be attractive to some and unimportant to others. As a business owner you need to stick to your beliefs, because if you don't you'll quickly become disenchanted with your business and lose the passion, drive and enthusiasm that keep you going.

In order to help you define the attributes which will become your culture and values, first you should consider what is really important to you. Answer the following questions, honestly, and keep those answers as this will be the basis of defining the culture:

- What are your values and beliefs?
- How will they shape your business?
- What ethical areas are a no-go – where are your boundaries?
- What do you want your business to 'stand for' – does it have a 'message'?

Whatever your answers, the outcome will be a set of clearly defined boundaries. Your values and beliefs will become the culture and values of the business you build. There are no right or wrong answers, but your answers will have an impact on every aspect of the business – the way it is run, the decisions you take.

Having a clear statement about your ethics is very important to retailers – slightly less of an issue if you're selling services to the retailer directly, but it will still always be part of a supplier selection process regardless of whether you are a services or product supplier. The reason that this is of particular importance when you are selling your goods through a retailer is because you have to consider the importance of consumer opinion. If a retailer is seen to be working with suppliers/brands that have 'a bad name' or are found to have unethical practices, it can cause tremendous harm to the retailer, who will often get the blame (as the brand facing the consumer), even when it was their supplier that was at fault. If you want to sell to retailers your business will come under some scrutiny with regard to ethical, environmental, equality and other policies. If you have that in mind when defining your culture, values and ethics at the outset you'll be in a strong position to demonstrate how you deal with the 'thorny issues' and why your business will not be the kind of supplier that brings negative consumer opinion to the retailer's door!

I am sure you will recall how several retailers over the years have had considerable negative PR owing to their supply chains not being as ethical as perhaps consumers would like. Some very high-profile cases have included M&S, Primark and Nike. Claims were made that there was use of child labour in their suppliers' factories. Some of the claims were discredited, others were addressed, *all* caused immediate and negative press and consumer reaction towards the retailer. The sales lost when something like that hits the headlines can't ever be recovered and the retailer's losses can run to millions. They certainly won't risk working with a supplier whose culture, values and ethics have even a sniff of a question mark... and that's why you should take time to focus on this.

Finally, and on a more positive note, culture, values and ethics can have a positive effect on loyalty. Think of a business you feel an affinity towards – a business you'd prefer to be loyal to even if they weren't perhaps the cheapest or most convenient. Can you think about the reasons why? Reflect on that. Often consumers are determinedly loyal to certain brands and the reasons appear vague; they may answer 'well I just like them' or 'I can trust them'. Underlying that is some attribute of attraction that has made a consumer develop an emotional (as opposed to a rational) connection with the brand. Brands and businesses, like individuals, project a 'personality' – successful brands are able to communicate their personality through their actions and behaviours. They attract people who share similar culture, values and ethics, because people like people who are similar to them, and they like organizations which are similar to them too – it's a key element of loyalty.

Think about the three well-known retailers listed below – they have some very specific personality traits that are made a core part of their PR and marketing campaigns. These traits attract customers to them and help them to secure their ongoing loyalty and trust:

- M&S: With Plan A (because there is no Plan B...) M&S resonates with all those who are conscious about environmental impacts and sustainability. Likely to be attracting a more middle-class, higher-income customer who can spend a little more but who also wants to be seen to be doing their bit for the environment. Shopping in M&S enables them to be more 'green' without having to actually make too many sacrifices.

- Co-op: A business owned by their members, their focus is on the local community. Their marketing is attractive to people who feel that they should shop local to support their local economy and to those who want to belong to, and contribute to, the community. Chances are that the Co-op attracts customers who value strong links to the local area and who believe that a thriving country is made up of many thriving communities.

- John Lewis: A business owned by their partners, every employee has a long-term vested interest in the success of the company and customers know that this means the service standards are world class. While not necessarily at the upper end of luxury, the loyal customer knows that John Lewis values a long-term, trust-based relationship with them and won't let little niggles/ issues deter them from their dedication to supporting the brand. Customers who shop with John Lewis feel valued and remain loyal because they appreciate the reassurance of buying from a brand that strives to deliver the very highest service standards, and knowing that if they do encounter problems these will be swiftly and politely resolved.

I chose these three because people do understand what they are all about and they are great examples of how to leverage the personality (culture, values, ethics) of a business to engage a loyal customer base.

So, before moving on to the next part, please spend a little time jotting down your thoughts about your business culture, values and ethics – these will evolve into your key statements about what you stand for and will help you to define your policies in the future.

Having determined the foundations with your mission, culture, values and ethics, we're next going to move on to review how you 'communicate' with the world, and for that we'll explore positioning.

Determining your positioning

So, what is positioning?

Positioning is a way you can describe how you would be considered, relative to your competitive set, by potential customers or in fact by anyone who 'notices' your brand. It is important to be realistic about your competitive set – this could otherwise be so diverse a group as to make any analysis of positioning an onerous exercise. Instead, be sensible about who your competition are and make some judgements about which brands are the most probable alternatives that your customer would choose if they did not choose your business.

As with the mission statement, if you are selling a product through retailers for an end consumer you should look at this through the eyes of the consumer. If you are selling a product or service to the retailer for their internal use then obviously you need to consider the retailer as your direct customer:

- If you are selling through a retailer ask yourself: what are the most likely alternatives that your ideal *consumer* group might consider when planning to purchase what *you* offer?

- If you are selling to a retailer consider: who are the most likely alternatives that your ideal *retailer* would consider as suppliers?

The assessment of your positioning is based on the consideration of how you would rate versus the relevant competition in four key areas – product, price, presentation and service.

Positioning enables you to have not only a greater clarity of what you offer but also a better understanding of how you are differentiated from your competition. Later, in Chapter 5 on competition, we'll look more closely at competitive sets and how to really analyse and understand them.

There is another interesting aspect of positioning – it leads your potential customer to make judgements about your brand even if they have no prior experience of being your customer. Think about this for a moment and reflect on some brands you know of – I'll give an example with some hotel chains. You may not have stayed in each of these hotel chains but from what you 'know' of them, from their positioning, you'll have formed an opinion of price, value, quality, service and desirability:

- Travelodge;
- Hilton;
- Marriot;
- Premier Inn.

Your opinion, as a potential consumer, has been influenced by everything that they 'share' with the world. From their branding to their marketing materials, the locations of their premises to the style of their buildings, everything that's 'communicated' to the potential customer contributes to forming an opinion as to what it would be like to be a customer of the brand, and what it would be reasonable to expect as a customer of the brand. This concept is explored further in the latter part of this chapter and also in Chapter 2 on presence. Essentially, what you as the business owner need to realize is that the words you use in marketing, the images/graphics/colours in your branding, your business location, what you wear, how you answer calls, and even the quality of your business cards, all are part of the outward representation of your brand. This all contributes to creating an impression in the 'eye of the beholder' about your business. Thus the four elements of positioning – product, price, presentation and service – all work together in harmony to attract (or repel) those customers we're planning to attract (or repel).

Let's look at how.

Breaking down the four elements of positioning

When it comes to positioning there are four elements that work together; my terminology is 'product, price, presentation and service'. I've seen other wording used in different business texts – it doesn't matter really, the crux is that you know what it means and therefore you can use it:

1 **Product**: what the end customer gets. This includes the features and benefits, the ingredients. It generically covers physical goods as well as services.

2 **Pricing**: what you are asked to pay for the product. Self-explanatory; when price is considered in the context of product and service delivery, a perception of value, or not, is created.

3 **Presentation**: the outward impression of the brand on the world. This includes, as listed above, words you use in marketing, the images/graphics/colours in your branding, your business location, what you wear, how you answer calls, and even the quality of your business cards – everything that the public can see of your brand, right down to the quality of the website or the styling of the packaging. This all gives an impression, a 'feeling' for what being a customer of the brand will be like. This is an area where brands can go horribly wrong as the outward representation makes implied promises to customers, which is why we're specifically going to look at this in the next section of the chapter.

4 **Service**: the way your customers are treated. This is beyond the 'hello, can I help you?' service that you may be used to getting. This is all about the extra benefits you get when you buy a product – things like the length of warranty or free delivery. This is to do with the whole purchasing experience, including after-sales service.

As I said before, it's not strictly about any one element; it's about all four working together. It's the relationship between all four elements of positioning that give the overall impression of the brand. If you are going to present a congruent and profitable brand you need to make sure that all four elements of positioning are in alignment.

There is a model I find very useful, called 'the arrows' – you may have come across it before, as it is quite widely used. In Figure 1.3 there are five brands, A–E. You will see that brands A–C have one or more 'arrows' out of alignment. There are issues with performance in brands A–C. Brands D and E are both doing very well.

FIGURE 1.3 The 'arrows' approach to understanding positioning

Brand	Product	Price	Presentation	Service	Status
A	↑	↓	↑	↑	Brand struggling to make a profit
B	↓	↑	↓	↓	Brand struggling to convert sales
C	↓	↑	↑	↑	Brand that gets a lot of returns
D	↑	↑	↑	↑	Brand doing well
E	↓	↓	↓	↓	Brand doing well

Looking in a bit more detail at each of these, brand A seems to be competing on price and yet investing in high-end product, presentation and service. Sometimes when the price is too low it actually puts off customers, who think 'something isn't quite right'. If you have a higher-end product it needs a higher price tag to be congruent. Stella Artois uses the strapline 'reassuringly expensive'; bear that in mind – it's a very clever use of language *and* it's why, when you have a higher-end positioning, you really should not attempt to compete on price. Clearly brand A will struggle to make a profit; they don't charge enough for each sale they make, and sales will be suppressed owing to customers not getting reassurance from the price.

Brand B, on the other hand, is overpricing. It has a lower-end product, presentation and service and is trying to overcharge its customers. People may be drawn to the brand assuming that, from the product or presentation, it will be a cheap option, but will not purchase when they see the price, as it will not represent value to them.

Brand C is leading customers to expect a quality product – the price, presentation and service all imply that the product is equally high-end. It isn't though, and when it does sell items it will get a high level of returns or complaints because the expectation of a quality item, for a higher price from a brand that is positioned at the higher end, has not been met.

Brands D and E are both successful – doing well – and although polar opposites, with one being all arrows up, higher-end, and one being all arrows down, lower-end, they have alignment and so in the eyes of the customer it's all 'congruent'.

So, bearing this in mind, consider these questions:

- Can you see how you could use positioning to benefit your business?

- Have you got any arrows out of alignment as it stands now?

- If you were to improve any aspect of your business, could you increase your prices, increase your attractiveness to customers and thus improve your profitability?

Reflect on your mission and who you ideally want to attract as customers and make sure your positioning fits and that your arrows are aligned.

Think of the brands D and E and reflect back on the example of hotels – Hilton could be brand D and Premier Inn brand E. Both are successful because both have clear distinction in their positioning that leads the customers to have expectations about each brand, which the brand lives up to. That leads us into my 'positioning mantra'. I believe that when customers feel they have been given bad service it can often link back to positioning. Through positioning, and often without realizing it, you are making promises to your customers about what they should expect the experience of being your customer to be like, so I hope you remember that:

> When your brand makes promises, implied or explicit, these set expectations with your customer.
>
> If you fail to deliver on those promises, you will fail to deliver the expected customer experience.

I'd like to share an example of a client I worked with whose pricing was too low, so, like brand A above, it was making a few low-profit sales. I won't disclose the name of the brand, so we'll just call it brand A.

Brand A had developed a luxury product aimed at a very high-end market, the kind of people that go to country events such as Ascot, Henley, Wimbledon – the well-heeled who like to be seen in all the right places, with the right friends, and with the right accessories. The product looked expensive, it was costly to manufacture, and all of the other attributes of the positioning were very clearly 'upward arrows'. The price was slightly low. A major and prestige department store wanted to stock the item but wanted to almost double the recommended retail price (RRP) of the item. When I first met brand A it was terribly concerned about this. It told me that its rate of sale was already very low – surely doubling the price would mean it sold none at all? The department store required brand A to ensure that the advertised price on its own website (where it sold the product direct to consumers) was aligned to the price that the department store would be selling the item for from its stores. A perfectly reasonable request, and one that would avoid any customer disharmony if an item purchased in-store was later found to be available online for a far lower price.

My answer to the dilemma faced by brand A was all about positioning. By increasing the price it would make a considerable amount more profit on its unit sales *and* it would achieve that 'reassuringly expensive' status which would be very important to its ideal customer.

Tentatively, and with much coaching, brand A agreed to increase its prices. What happened next was amazing – sales began to increase! It even sold several units to a senior representative of the royal family! Since then it has had enquiries from a number of dignitaries about purchasing several units to give as gifts to foreign ambassadors and the like. It was incredible. I expected that bringing the price positioning into a congruent alignment with product, presentation and service would benefit brand A, but of course we couldn't have predicted how successful it would be, nor how soon after increasing the price it would happen.

Now brand A makes more than double the cash margin per unit sold than it did prior to making the changes *and* it is selling more units. A fantastic outcome and proof that, even in a contracted economy, when a product is clearly desirable and well positioned it will still attract the ideal customer.

That wraps up the section on positioning; I think we agree it is important to get it right. Next we'll look in more detail at the presentation aspect of your positioning, focusing on how, when it comes to 'punching above your weight', professionally designed logos, brochures, business cards, documentation and any other materials you may give out to clients and potential clients really can make a difference to how they perceive your brand.

Your brand's visual identity

Linked to all of the above, and explicitly the 'presentation' aspect of positioning, your branding is the visual 'description' of the business – colour evokes feeling, design evokes emotion. You have to ensure that the visual identity you choose for your business is positioned for the right audience. Furthermore, just because you might be a small business now, I would advocate planning ahead and developing the brand you intend to be, not necessarily designing it around what you are now. It's just like the saying 'dress for the job you want, not the job you have got' – you have to feel proud of your branding, and your branding needs to make potential customers think you're a serious contender.

However, unless you are a competent graphic designer, this is one area where I would wholly recommend you invest in some expert help – there is nothing more off-putting to a major corporate buyer than a 'homemade' look and feel to a logo, a brochure or a business card. It sets alarm bells ringing – 'if this business can't afford a decent designer and some quality printing, if they cut corners on that, then what else are they cutting corners on?'

When it comes to briefing a designer you will need to give them lots of information about your business – your mission, culture, values, ethics and positioning will all be very useful to help 'set the scene' as to what your business is about, what message it needs to convey and to whom. Some designers will ask you to put ideas together of brands you love or would aspire to be like – it helps them to understand where you are coming from in a more visual way. With this in mind, it is worth just spending a little time now to consider the following:

- What brands do you love, and why?
- What is it you identify with?
- Are they memorable, instantly recognizable?
- What 'attributes' of these brands would you like to carry forward into your own brand?
- What brands do you aspire to be most like?

The visual aspect of branding really works hand in hand with all the other elements of your business personality – the mission, culture, ethics and positioning which will attract some customers and repel others. Your visual identity is a key element of driving brand loyalty; your customer needs the ability to recognize your brand instantly. That may sound 'fluffy' but it can add commercial value to your business. Don't forget that when businesses are valued for sale, one element that is considered is 'brand equity' – that's how valuable the actual brand is considered to be in the market. Don't for one moment think that investment in this is a waste of money; it's one area you can't afford to get wrong because it's all about first impressions, which leads us neatly into how to use your visual identity to create those all-important first impressions.

Deployment of branding

It's off-putting for a major corporate to see poorly designed, poorly implemented branding, so the first rule of your branding is to ensure consistency of deployment. That means using the same format of images, the same colour palette, the same fonts, the same document templates. After that it's back to positioning – consider your business card, brochure or exhibition stand to be your presentation and make sure that you are deploying a congruent message. However, even if you are a lower-end brand there are some things to avoid. One bugbear of mine is the free, template-design business cards you can get printed for minimal cost – they look and feel cheap. To the receiver it feels like little effort or attention to detail has been expended. Consider that while you may have a lower-end product and thus a brand identity which evokes a more 'budget' feel, you don't want to be seen as unprofessional or cheap. There is a subtle difference, but I can assure you that if the managing director of easyJet handed you a card it would look like it had been professionally designed and it would be printed on quality card. While the brand image is 'budget' the business is still highly professional, so don't fall into the trap of allowing down arrows in the positioning to become down arrows when it comes to your professionalism! Investment in professional, quality materials will reap rewards; retailers will take you more seriously, you won't appear to be the kind of business that cuts corners and you'll be more memorable. You don't need to go mad – work out what you need initially and then start with the bare essentials – you can always add to that as required. It's imperative that you allow for both brand design and deployment costs in your business plan when starting up.

Some of the things you really will need are:

- logo;
- colour palette;
- standard font.

Some things you'll need over time are:

- website design;
- business cards;
- brochure/flyer or other 'leave-behind' materials;
- exhibition stand (if you intend to go to trade shows);

- packaging samples (if relevant to what you intend to sell);
- PowerPoint template, for presentations;
- Word template, for proposal documents.

As we work through the Pitch Big part you're likely to have more ideas about what you'll need to have to engage effectively with the retailers, present to them, and leave a lasting impression. You can then add to the list above, making sure you think through what is a *must*-have and what is just a 'nice to have'.

Wrapping up

In this chapter we have looked at the important part that identity plays in enabling your business to 'look big'. You should now be clear on how to create and develop:

- your mission statement;
- your culture, values and ethics;
- your positioning.

Building from these foundations you should also now appreciate the importance of the creation and deployment of your visual identity, considering how perception of your brand is influenced by your brand image. You now have the ability to review your branding and ask yourself:

- Is your brand identity congruent with your mission, positioning and values?
- Does your brand make you 'look big'?
- Is your branding appropriately and consistently deployed?

The branding elements link tightly to the next chapter, on presence. We'll look at how aspects of your business presence are closely connected to the deployment of your visual identity. So, taking forward everything we've learnt about your business identity, let's move on to the next element of 'looking big', your business presence.

02 Presence

Introduction

This chapter will look at your business presence, both in the physical world and in the online world. We will be focusing on:

- **First impressions**: considering what you can do to ensure that the first impression anyone who comes into contact with your business has is a good one. We'll delve into:
  - what kind of business location you should have;
  - how to ensure you never mess up an important call.
- **Your online presence**: making sure that you have a congruent brand identity and narrative online and that you're taking advantage of the different options available to you to increase your online presence. We'll consider your 'findability' and how being easily found online adds to your credibility in the eyes of a retail buyer. We'll look at:
  - protecting your brand name online through securing domains and social media accounts;
  - how to ensure your website is comparable to, if not better than, those presented by your competition;
  - 'findability'; making sure that when a retail buyer goes looking for you they find the content you want them to see.

The whole purpose of this chapter is to ensure that no matter how a retail buyer comes across your brand, in the physical or online worlds, they'll get a great first impression that gives them certainty that you're the kind of professional business they'd be confident to do business with.

Moments of truth...

It is said that people form judgements about others within a few seconds. The same is true in business, and it's true whether that point of contact is face to face, on e-mail, over the phone or online. If your ideal buyer gets the feeling that you're not a serious business then you're very unlikely ever to be successful selling to them.

It's important to remember this when you're getting the basics in place – if you're starting up, it's relatively easy to get things right first time; if you're established, you may want to review your business's presence by putting yourself in the shoes of a potential customer and seeing what it 'feels' like. You may notice there are some improvements that could really benefit you.

In customer services training you'll often hear the point of interaction between a potential customer and a business called a 'moment of truth' – the reason is that the customer's judgement is not based on all of the evidence you may have to prove your credibility or quality. In that split second, that moment, the judgement is based on the customer's own specific experience of dealing with you. While everything else about your brand can reinforce a great experience, if customers have a bad experience with you then you'll have a battle on your hands to win them over; perhaps they'll always have a nagging doubt in their minds about your brand. That's why, silly as it may initially seem, you do need to invest time and money into some of these ingredients to ensure that as many of those 'moments of truth' as possible are excellent.

The moments of truth, touch points, can be diverse – they include anything that could impact on the first impression that your business gives to an external third party. The most likely would be (but are not limited to):

- your office address;
- your phone number;
- your business card;
- your brochure, or any printed materials that you may send out, use at a trade show, or leave behind after a meeting;

- your website, or any online content about you that a retail buyer might come across;
- your e-mail address;
- your social media;
- your call answering.

Test it out on the table shown in Figure 2.1 – using the list above once again but now considering how you'd feel about buying from company A or company B if you were a senior buyer for a major retail chain.

FIGURE 2.1   Exploring the impact of 'moments of truth'

Customer touch point	Company A	Company B
Your office address – home address vs. professional business premises	A residential address is clearly used for Companies House registration and a PO Box for correspondence.	The business is registered at a professional premises; while it may be a serviced office, there is a 'real place' (not a PO Box) for correspondence.
Your phone number	There is only a mobile number presented.	Three numbers are offered – a Lo-call/Free number, a 'normal' landline number (for overseas/mobile phone users) and an additional mobile phone number.
Your business card	The card is flimsy and looks cheaply designed – there's the logo of a free online card design service on the back. The contact details on the card are minimal.	The card feels 'solid' and it looks well designed. The brand's visual identity (logo, colours and fonts) is used on the card and the contact details are comprehensive.

FIGURE 2.1   *continued*

Customer touch point	Company A	Company B
Your brochure, or any printed materials that you may send out, use at a trade show or leave behind after a meeting	The materials are just on standard paper, probably printed in-house. There is an inconsistent use of the brand colours, fonts and styling. The copy is not well structured. It looks 'homemade' and certainly not well thought out. All the key information *is* included, but your gut feeling when you are handed the materials is: 'Is that it?!'	Materials are well designed and may be in different shapes, styles, formats. The brand image is evident at first glance. They are eye-catching, easy to read and the copy is well structured to draw attention to the most important messages. The materials feel 'substantial' and there is no doubt that a great deal of thought and effort went into design and production.
Your website, or any online content about you that a retail buyer might come across	The website looks homemade, is slow to load and several pages are 'under construction'. The brand colours, logo and fonts aren't consistent. There are visual issues with the site – perhaps the menus 'jump' from page to page – it doesn't look slick. Copy is poorly written and it's hard to find the information you need. Worse, you can't find any contact details! This website just looks cheap and badly constructed. You know that someone has not really invested in it.	The website is well presented, fast to load and complete. The brand is instantly recognizable, with fonts, logos and colours used consistently. The navigation is clear, easy to understand and helps you find out what you need. It is well written and takes the browser through to clear contact details – with options to call, e-mail or complete an enquiry form. Evidently time and money were spent on it.

FIGURE 2.1   *continued*

Customer touch point	Company A	Company B
Your e-mail	The e-mail address is a generic one, not linked to the website domain, eg company.name@gmail.com (or AOL, Hotmail etc).	The e-mail address is domain based and function or person specific, eg accounts@business.com or name.surname@business.com
	The e-mail itself has no auto-signature or it says 'sent from my iPhone'. It is in plain text and content may be grammatically incorrect or include spelling errors.	The e-mail includes a professional auto-signature and privacy statement. The formatting includes company fonts, colours and logo. Copy is checked before sending, and spelling and grammar errors corrected, so the received e-mail is always well constructed and error free.
Your social media	The company Facebook page, blog, Twitter account, LinkedIn group etc are incomplete and seemingly unused. Last status updates on social media seem to reflect more the business owner's personal life than brand messaging. It looks ill thought out and thrown together.	The company has created on-brand social media with logos, styles and colours in place. Where media exists it is used consistently and the content is relevant, on-brand messaging. Evidently the use of social media has been well thought out, the company has a presence where you would expect, and is using it in a professional and appropriate manner.

FIGURE 2.1   *continued*

Customer touch point	Company A	Company B
Your call answering	Calls are picked up and answered 'hello' (nothing more) and as the only number was a mobile phone it's often difficult to hear the person speaking. If not picked up, the calls go through to a standard mobile phone network provider voicemail message. It feels like a business with only one resource as there's only the mobile number offered.	Calls are picked up within three rings and answered politely: 'Good morning, [company name], how can I help you' or similar. Calls can be put through to the right person, or occasionally that person answers. Messages are taken carefully, with fully detailed notes, and you have confidence that the message will be passed on. It feels like this business has invested in administrative/support staff and is a professional team.

Obviously you'd choose company B – but when it comes to your business, and the first impression you give, how many of the above areas are more like company A? If *that* aspect is the 'moment of truth' for your ideal retail buyer, you'll have an uphill struggle to win them back once you've given a poor first impression.

There will be more elements that affect first impressions; the above just gives you a flavour of the more obvious ones. I am sure you'd agree that whether you like it or not, judgements are made on first impressions (and are hard to change) and *all* these elements will have an impact.

So, exploring this a little further, we're going to dig deeper into the physical aspects of your presence – we'll talk about the importance of a professional business address, your phone number and how calls are handled, and your printed materials. After that, we'll look at your online presence, which will include your domain name, e-mail address and all other 'virtual' presence you have.

Your physical presence

Business name

Let's start at the beginning – your business name. You need to spend time thinking about a name that is memorable but also making checks as to what's already in use.

In the UK (there will be other similar services in other countries) you can use a free web-check service with Companies House – the registrar of all UK limited companies, public companies and limited partnerships. This check will show you if the name you want is available. If the name you want appears to be available, you need to check a few other places before making your choice.

Step 2 is to check on the Intellectual Property Office website – to see if anyone has a brand registered that is similar to (or the same as) your ideal company name. You don't want to create a business name that is already a protected brand – you'll be told to cease trading very quickly and may also get a legal case against you for using another brand's name!

If both checks seem to indicate that your business name is a good one, the final check should be to actually search for the planned name online – see what references exist that could be using the same name. There are several acronyms, for instance, that have dual meaning – ATCM is the Association of Town Centre Management but it is also the Association of Traditional Chinese Medicine! One of my clients was about to launch a lingerie brand under the name 2BU, only to discover that the top Google search for this name was a lesbian, gay and transgender group! My client didn't want to be confused with a pre-existing brand or organization and so quickly renamed its company. It's even happened to pop bands – in the UK in 2011 on the popular singing contest *The X Factor*, a group was created out of several solo female singers. They called the group Rhythmix. A few weeks later it transpired that Rhythmix was already the name of a charity and so the band 'rebranded' to become known as Little Mix. They went on to win the contest, but the name change was obviously unsettling for them. The researchers on the TV show should really have done a better job for them!

When you've checked out all avenues and are happy with the name, you then need to decide what kind of business you become. This would be a good time to research your options and to think once again about the impression given to an outsider. The usual option in the UK is to become a private limited company (Company Name Ltd), as this protects the owners from liabilities that the company takes on. There are other structures – plenty of information is available online so you can decide the one that fits your business model best.

Now you have a name and you know how you want to be 'structured'; the next step is to form the company officially – and once you do, remember that your company becomes a new legal entity that has obligations and duties. You should get some professional advice (an accountant or legal professional can help) unless you are certain you know what you are doing. As it is different for each individual business I would not advise going forward without some validation or support from an expert in this area – there is too much to lose.

Finally, one more consideration when it comes to naming: if your product has a different name (brand or otherwise) from the name of the business, you also need to ensure that this isn't being used by any other company or brand. Do the same checks. You don't necessarily need to own the limited company name for additional brands, although you can secure these if you wish, keeping them dormant, in order to protect your additional brand names.

Your business address

Once you have decided on a name, when it comes to registering your company you will be required to provide an address which will be used as the company's registered address with Companies House. Smaller businesses typically use a home address or an accountant's address. Bear in mind, though, that retail buyers can do a simple Companies House online check (as you did on available company names) and if they see that your registered address is a domestic address it will immediately shout 'small' to them.

There are serviced offices which offer smaller businesses the right to use their address for both company registration and receiving correspondence. In fact, one of my businesses, Albans Office Space, does this. This service is called a 'virtual office' and it's a great way for smaller businesses to appear to have a prestige or professional location anywhere they want for a limited amount of money. Many of these office providers can also provide meeting rooms, use of work space on a temporary or permanent basis, and a range of secretarial services (including call handling). Using a facility such as this is a great way to look big, with the added bonus that it protects your home address from being shared in the public domain through things like the Companies House databases. Personally, as a director of a small business, that's the more comforting aspect to me, the added benefit of keeping my private details private. So do bear that in mind when you're weighing up the costs versus benefits of using a virtual office or similar – not only are you showing potential buyers that you want to project a professional image but you're also avoiding any risk of someone connected to work arriving at your home!

There is a great deal of flexibility when it comes to picking an ideal address for your business. You need to do a bit of thinking about this; you should be looking ahead to when you are a bigger business. Ask yourself where you ideally want to appear to be located. When your business grows, and you need staff and premises where they can work, would you be able to take on premises either at the preferred virtual office location or in that town at least? Office moves, even virtual office moves, can be costly, as you need to change all references to your business address – with customers, suppliers, Companies House; online content and also printed materials could become obsolete. It's best to choose an address that gives you longevity, at least until the cost of updating cards is a minor concern in the context of your accelerated growth!

Your business phone

It may seem that the phone is of little significance, but remember, it's a key first impression.

If you have a fixed office premises then you can contract a more 'traditional' phone service through a telecoms provider. Alternatively, technology such as VoIP (voice over IP) phone systems enable you to buy into services for a relatively low fee and are great for dynamic businesses, as you can use VoIP services anywhere that you've got an internet connection. When arranging your phone lines and planning how you will manage calls, you might also consider a call handling service. Often they can provide you with the numbers and their only charges are per call received. Some charge per call, others per second, so do your price comparisons and look at the different options/packages available.

A number of call handling services now operate 24/7 and offer support for online businesses. If you also sell products through your own e-commerce system, a provider like this may be greatly beneficial to you. Their service means that your customers can place an order, check the status of an order, arrange a return, or register a complaint 24/7 – and a trained team of customer service advisers can give you that support, often at just a small price per call. For most small businesses there is no way that they could employ resources to cover 24/7 call answering for the price you'd pay to outsource it, so I'd wholly recommend that you take a closer look at this option.

Whatever route you choose to take, you need to be planning ahead – as with a change in address, a change in phone number has implications and is extra work and cost that you can avoid if you invest a bit of time thinking about what you *will* need in the mid-term and not just getting something that 'will do for now'.

So, you have a company name, a registered address and phones all sorted out – that gives you the content you need to create business cards and other printed materials, so let's take a look at that aspect now.

Your brochure, business card and other promotional media

Recently I had a conversation with a client who didn't really understand why they needed to invest in the design, copy-writing and print of a leave-behind at a client meeting. Their point was valid in some respects:

> Why should I spend all that money on developing something to leave with a person I've just met? Surely now we've met in person the relationship has gone beyond the marketing materials and the leave-behind is just a waste?

That's probably the case if you are selling a product to a small retailer, talking to the decision maker, when there are no other influencers involved. Still, it's good to leave something behind as a visual, physical reminder of you and your business.

When it comes to bigger companies a leave-behind is crucial. There will be several parties involved in the decision to buy (that is true whether it be products or services) and the leave-behind enables the person you met, who we hope will be 'on your side', to update their colleagues (others influential to the decision to progress with your company) about your business. If you've left a well-structured pack that enables them to explain to colleagues what you offer, with some great visuals, it's almost as good as you being there yourself. Put it this way: if you lost a possible five- or six-figure contract because you didn't create a leave-behind pack, how would you feel?!

This is an area where you need really to focus: you need to be sure that the copy, images, design, layout, style, and even paper quality and finish are giving the right impression about your brand. It's not just about your content, it's the whole package. A good designer will be able to give you some ideas about what your finished product could look like, and when you've decided what 'structure' (as in booklet, flyer, folder, brochure, what size etc) you prefer, they can begin to design the content for you – using your brand colours, fonts, logos and styles as well as any relevant images you have. One thing to be mindful of when choosing a format for your leave-behind is that some types of document can have a very high minimum order quantity, 1,000 for example, and if you do order lower quantities you end up paying a very high per-unit cost. This is because some leave-behind packs require special 'cutting' to produce the shape/size you like. When you are working with the designer, ask them to help you select a structure of document that is going to be less costly to produce. That will help you avoid the nasty surprise when the printer tells you what the costs to print will be!

During the design process you will need to supply the copy, working with the designer to help lay it out around the visuals. You should pick out the key messages that help someone looking at the document to focus on what you want to draw their attention to. It can be a slow process, often frustrating when you feel 'it's not quite right but I don't know why!', but when you get to that moment of 'yes, *that* is what I want people to remember about my business' you'll feel great about the leave-behind and eager to actually give it to someone!

Having sorted out all your materials in the 'real world' we'll now move on to consider your online presence, your 'virtual world'!

Your online presence

Google claims that by 2020 over 90 per cent of *all* purchasing decisions will be influenced by content found online. That's not just consumer purchases either, it includes business to business as well. I actually think that's a conservative estimate. I can already see in my behaviour and in the behaviour of others just how influential online content is. By way of example I'll share a story which really reinforced this for me:

> Several years ago I was speaking to a gentleman who used Albans Office Space for client meetings – he lived just two minutes' walk away. One day I saw him walk past the office carrying a roll of carpet on his shoulder. When he next came into the office I was chatting to him and I commented on this. It turned out that he had bought it in an end-of-season sale and now needed a carpet fitter. I knew a fitter, a neighbour as it happened, and he'd fitted carpets in my house. I suggested the fitter to him. The response was a surprise; without stopping to think he asked me 'does he have a website?' Now I was talking about a carpet fitter I knew, a neighbour, who had done good work for me. In the past, this sort of word-of-mouth recommendation would have been more than enough and yet now the potential customer wanted to look at a website.

What I realized was that a website had become, as a minimum, a comfort factor in the purchasing decision. The ability of the potential buyer to look at a website, see contact details and possibly some images, seemed to make the service provider more 'genuine', thus influencing the purchasing decision. It was as though the credibility of the service provider was questionable unless they had a website/online presence.

Have you made similar demands yourself? Did you feel more confident buying from someone simply because you were able to find them online? If decisions about purchasing such simple things as the services of a local carpet fitter, who had already been recommended to you, are influenced by online content, imagine just how important it is for *your* business! You need to influence the retail buyer and all the stakeholders. Your online content needs to give them considerable confidence in you, your business and your ability to service their requirements. Therefore, the more quality content you can present, the better.

What *is* 'quality content' online? How do you build an online presence? Essentially your online presence draws on elements of your visual identity and your business narrative. The quality comes from the consistency of brand presentation, how readily content can be found and how easy it is for a browser to navigate your content. Time-poor corporate buyers can incorrectly judge a smaller business if they don't get the right impression from its online content.

In addition, there are areas of online presence that are more about protecting your brand than specifically influencing a buyer. Take social media, for instance: you don't want someone to set up a Twitter account with your business identity – they may share content that is damaging to your brand and it could appear to have come from you. The brand protection aspect of your online presence is important in order to avoid negative influence.

Next we'll look at how you can best present your brand online. We'll look at your website, your social media presence and your own online profile as the business owner/founder.

Your website domain

I'm not going to give you a lesson in best-practice website design, build or optimization – that's probably three more books and frankly my husband is the expert in all that stuff! The purpose of this section is to look at how your website contributes to your presence, to helping you to look big, and to giving that all-important right first impression.

The starting place, and tied into the selection of the company name, is to secure the right domain(s). Your primary domain, the one at which your website is found, does impact on your 'findability' in search – not only the words that form the domain but the suffix (.co.uk, .com, .net etc), so choose it wisely or get some advice from a search marketing expert. You also need to consider securing additional domains, those very similar to your company or brand name. This is part of your brand protection process; it means that you avoid the possibility of another party buying domains similar to yours and setting up copycat websites. This is a very murky area of law, although in the UK there is an organization which was established to help with domain name disputes. Generally the best approach is to secure the domains that are most like your brand name in order to avoid there ever being any need to deal with an issue in the future.

Domains can be registered for less than £10, and often for an initial two years, so even if you choose to secure 10 variations it's not a massive outlay to protect your business in the future. You will need to renew domains in order to retain ownership, so that's one to plan ahead and budget for.

Your e-mail address

Once you've chosen a suitable main domain, the one that your website will be presented on, you will be able to set up professional e-mail addresses. Unless you are fairly technical you may need the support of an IT expert to create the e-mail addresses you require (remember that you can have function-specific as well as named addresses – eg accounts@..., enquiries@..., customerservices@..., Name. surname@...). Creating e-mail addresses is one thing, but ensuring they route through to the appropriate person is another – hence you may need an IT expert to do the set-up and you may be advised to use a small business server to manage your e-mails as well. All of these things come at a cost, but are important to enable you to grow efficiently and to look big from the outset. Avoid sending e-mails that are on 'generic' domains – these are the free services such as Gmail, Hotmail, AOL etc – it looks unprofessional.

Once you have your new domain-based e-mail accounts created, you can use e-mail software, like Microsoft Outlook for instance, to set up your formatting, auto-signature and also out-of-office auto-replies.

Your company website

You've got a domain secured, and this is where you'll present your website, but as yet you don't have anything visible on the domain. You need to create a website that is technically accurate (program code errors can mean your website can't be interpreted by search engines, so it will drop down in search results), visually engaging (on-brand and easy to navigate) and well structured (not the same as navigation; this means how it is built and how elements of content are put together to ensure maximum opportunity with the search engines). You also need to ensure that the copy on the site is readable (think about the words used, the density, the flow and the layout – people classically skim-read websites, so you need to use headings to signpost key text that you want to draw attention to).

Your website in its entirety is more important to your business presence than any physical materials. It is available and visible to *all* users of the internet (including your competition), unlike physical materials which are only available to those to whom you distribute them.

When it comes to implementing the website, you need a designer to help you make it look great and a developer to create it. The developer essentially takes you from concepts and drawings to a live presence on the internet. You need to plan it all out in detail, everything from the layout on the page and the blocks of content to the menu format and links. A good starting point is to identify other websites that are perhaps similar to what you'd like – you can pick two or three websites if you can't find just one you most like – perhaps the main page layout is great on one site, the navigation and menus good on another, and perhaps you like the design and styling of a third. Research like this can help your designer to understand what you're trying to achieve and help your developer to guide you about what's most efficient when it comes to technical deployment.

Of course, in planning out your navigation and menus you have to consider the pages you want to have. What will they say? What are they for? Your website should serve a number of purposes:

1 To prove your credibility after you've already met someone and ideally to ensure that your business comes across as a better choice than your competition!

2 To provide a reference resource to those who may know you well but who want to refer back to your products and/or services.

3 To enable you to get found in search and to then take a browser through to an action.

So it's key to have an aim in mind for every page, and if you want to encourage action then the words you use and the visibility of such things as 'contact us' forms or phone numbers should be considered.

So, to sum up, the key considerations for your web design and content are:

- On-brand: it looks like your business; it represents your brand's visual identity.

- On-message: it sounds like your business; the copy and narrative represent the business effectively.

- Ease of navigation: it's easy to find information, it's easy to return to the home page.

- Clarity of content: it's easy to read and digest information; key messages are identifiable.

- It doesn't give too much away to the competition! There's enough to grab attention, but you're keeping your key information closely guarded, encouraging further contact for more details.

- Call to action: you have made it clear when a browser should make contact with you and you've made it easy for them to do so.

Next we'll look at how to improve your findability, because one of the most beneficial and value-adding uses of your website is attracting new enquiries from people who found you through search.

Search marketing

Search marketing is a complex area, it's regularly changing, and it's something even some of the biggest organizations will outsource to specialists. With that in mind, and in order to get your website found in search for the right phrases and by the right kind of people, you will almost certainly have to invest in specialist search marketing skills.

Beware of *any* website provider that tells you it's got 'SEO built in' (SEO – search engine optimization). It can't be! If a car dealer told you that your car had 'fuel built in' you'd know it was just marketing spin and probably expect just a tank full. You'd expect to refuel when it was empty. SEO is similar; it fuels the website and needs constant review and re-evaluation. Websites can be structured such that they are easier to apply search optimization techniques to, *but* they can't have SEO built in. SEO requires an understanding of your business marketing objectives and ideal customer, a great deal of research and analysis, and then some changes will probably be required to both the content as well as the back-end structure of the website (you will hear things such as titles, descriptions, meta-tags, image-tags, key content and headings mentioned). These are some of the things that a search marketing expert can improve on your website to increase its likelihood of appearing for certain search phrases. A bit like adding some fuel to an engine!

Only about 30 per cent of the impact of a good SEO process is about your website. The rest is a mixture of factors often called 'off-site SEO'. In very basic terms, because the internet is a web of information, the number of interconnections between pages on the web increases the apparent importance of a page in search. Traffic, bounce rate and a long, long list of other factors will also have an effect.

Your search marketing expert will help you to identify where opportunities lie for your business in search, what you need to focus on, and where it is simply not worth the effort (too heavily contested, dominated by mega-brands with mega-budgets etc). They'll also be able to advise on how to leverage content on other sites, such as blogs and social media, to help increase the number of relevant visitors to your website.

Your social media presence is important to your search marketing strategy as well as your brand protection. When it's all set up you can also add social links to your website, so it's an inclusive representation of your brand, offering all 'channels' for contact.

With that in mind, let's look at social media next.

Your social media presence

I'm not going to attempt to explain all the nuances of social media in this short section. I will, however, share some questions and thoughts with you for you to explore and consider with specific relevance to your business.

When I work with clients, social media is often an area of real concern. That's usually got more to do with lack of familiarity than complexity. I run a specific strategy workshop to help them figure out how they can use social media for the benefit of their business. In this session we work through a series of questions:

1 *Why* do you want to use social media for business – what is the purpose or objective?

2 *Who* do you want to engage or connect with via social media – who are the audience?

3 *What* kind of content do you plan to distribute – what content could you distribute that would attract the audience?

4 *When* will you distribute content – what frequency? Will it be influenced by calendar events?

5 *Where* should you distribute content – based on the output of the four earlier points, what media should you be using? What is priority?

6 *How* will you do it – automated/feeds, personally or a mixture? What skills do you need to get started?

From these questions we're quickly able to fine-tune a robust plan, just like any other project plan, which defines the purpose and the approach. If you spend some time considering each of the above questions it will help you to clarify what you should or should not be focusing on for your business's social media presence. You will need to take each question in sequence, as what you learn by answering the first will influence the answer to the next etc.

With regard to the different media available, there are a plethora of tools that essentially allow you and your brand to communicate via the social web. The most popular are Facebook, Twitter, LinkedIn, YouTube and blogs. In Figure 2.2 I review each of these popular social media tools in terms of pros and cons, with specific reference to your business. I've also briefly summarized the tool in case you are not familiar with it. This is not an exhaustive list, but it should help you select the media relevant to you in line with your answers to the six questions above.

FIGURE 2.2   Pros and cons of the more popular social media tools

Media	Description	Pros	Cons
Facebook	Social networking site for connecting with friends. Informal, very social, businesses that have a Facebook presence need to be mindful that this is a casual interaction, not a formal one. All kinds of media can be shared – your news, mood, images, videos, links – and there are lots of games and groups that make it even more focused on play rather than on work!	Great for engaging with consumers or even other people in business on a more social basis. You may well be able to engage end users of your product via Facebook to get useful feedback too. If you can be social in person then you can use Facebook!	You'll be highly unlikely to connect with retail buyers on Facebook. If your primary sales channel is business to business then, unless you're looking to engage the end user, it may take up a lot of your time for little benefit. You need at least to secure a Facebook page in your brand name, even if you don't plan to use it. This avoids the issue of it being unavailable should you decide to use it at a later date.
Twitter	Social media site where users 'follow' other users and share messages, tweets (which can contain links to websites, blogs, images etc) that are under 140 characters. Twitter is a mix of individuals chatting, professionals connecting, and brands sharing. It's also a great place to find the latest news.	Twitter enables you to follow a range of users that interest you. You can also search within Twitter to see if your brand name or business is referenced. This means you can acknowledge mentions and address issues in a very open environment. Other Twitter users may share your content so that all those following them can see it – therefore you have the opportunity to get your messaging amplified and engage an otherwise hard-to-reach audience.	It is easy to get disillusioned with Twitter; it takes some getting used to. You need to establish a 'tone of voice' for your business and that can be difficult. Once you get started the expectation of your followers is that you'll maintain your presence and so you need to allocate ongoing time to producing fresh content, which can be a drain on your resources. You need to secure Twitter identities for your brand, irrespective of whether you plan to use it as otherwise your name may be taken by a third party. This means that when you do want to use Twitter your brand name won't be available.

FIGURE 2.2 *continued*

Media	Description	Pros	Cons
LinkedIn	A networking site for business people – not really that social at all – it began life as a tool for professionals to share CV data. It now has much richer content and can be connected to blogs and Twitter. There are pages available for companies as well as groups, so it's very diverse. The users are mainly corporate professionals, although the number of business owners using LinkedIn is growing.	This tool is excellent for connecting with senior decision makers in major retail organizations, your target audience. You can create a company page, with products and services listed, and solicit recommendations – great to have the third-party endorsement. You can join groups both to share ideas and to learn from businesses similar to yours or to network online with other group members. We'll look at LinkedIn in more detail in the next chapter as it's all about establishing your professional expertise and credibility to encourage the right kind of people to connect with you.	LinkedIn comes from a history of headhunters using it to find people, so there is quite a sales ethos, and you can occasionally receive 'spam'. It is such a vast tool that it is easy to get 'lost'. As this is likely to be where your ideal buyer has a profile, you need to make sure you are very confident in using it in order to avoid any negative impact on your brand or on your chance of engaging your ideal contact. I've used LinkedIn since 2005, and found it very beneficial. I've included my top tips as a downloadable PDF in the resources area via **www.retailchampion. co.uk/selling-to-retailers/ resources**.

FIGURE 2.2 *continued*

Media	Description	Pros	Cons
YouTube	A video-sharing site that enables users to add video content, share content, create their own 'online TV channel' and comment on other video content by adding video or text-based responses. It's also a very useful site for hosting promotional video that you can then embed in your website.	A great place to host videos that can be embedded on your own website and bring your product or service to life a bit more, making your website more engaging. Videos filter through to Google search and can 'go viral' in that they can be rapidly shared by other users – this can be hugely beneficial to a brand in terms of extending their reach.	Very few cons I can think of! If used correctly there are limited risks and predominantly only benefits from using YouTube. The only real con is learning how to use it, how to set up a channel in your brand identity, and how to maintain fresh, up-to-date content.
Blog	Blog is short for web-log. This is essentially an easy-to-update website, the basic functionality of which is free to use. A blog enables users to post articles, opinion pieces and news, sharing their expertise/thoughts and inviting comment from those who have subscribed to the blog or from anyone who finds the blog in search.	Blogs are a great way to share a bit more of the personality and know-how of the key individual(s) of the business. Rather like your own online magazine, blogs are a great way for your brand to respond and react to relevant news or topical subjects without having to edit the main website. Blogs also attract a wide variety of search terms, which your search marketing expert can analyze to help you further increase your traffic for the terms that are likely to be most valuable to your business.	Like the other media, once you get started you have to make a commitment to keep it up. If you blog weekly and then stop, you'll lose much of the benefit. You need to be careful what you say; you are still representing your brand. You also need to manage feedback and comments, moderating what's posted and acknowledging it. It can take up a lot of time.

So based on what we have just covered, I'm sure you can see how important social media is in terms of brand protection, spreading the word about your business and connecting with all the right people.

Wrapping up

In this chapter we considered your business presence in both the physical and online worlds, and how that presence can create a good (or bad) first impression.

We have explored 'moments of truth' and highlighted some of the key areas to be mindful of when developing your business presence. Digging deeper into this, we've walked through aspects of the real-world presence:

- business name;
- business address;
- business phone;
- marketing materials.

And of the online world:

- domain names;
- e-mail addresses;
- business website;
- search marketing;
- business use of social media.

You should now feel confident in presenting a great first impression and have a clear list of actions to put in place in order to ensure that you look big.

In the next chapter we'll look at your people, specifically exploring the impression of your business that *they* can give. We'll also explore some aspects of social media in more detail – namely the importance of online personal profiles for key individuals in your business.

03 **People**

Introduction

In this final chapter of 'Look Big' we'll focus on people. We'll be looking at why people are so fundamental to your business, not just in the context of delivering its proposition but in terms of making it look big!

We'll discuss how to:

- leverage the expertise of your key people to give the impression of calibre and capability;
- use third-party testimonials about your people so that you can stand out as 'thought-leaders' or 'innovators' in your field;
- focus on your niche, diverting attention away from the size of your organization;
- balance being *the* expert in your niche with the risk of being considered too small to match *big* company requirements;
- make use of a 'virtual team' to add substance to your business early on.

This chapter will conclude the part on 'Look Big', so at the end there is an end-of-part checklist for you to go through. You can use this to review your business and determine your action plan for this part.

People buy from people...

This is a well-known saying, and it's true. While all of the identity and presentation stuff is great, and it certainly makes your potential client feel 'safe' with your business, when it comes to the crunch it all boils down to your people doing the deal with the client's people. Therefore you must not underestimate the significance of surrounding yourself with the right individuals, not just to make your business look big but to make it look exceptional!

Retailer buyers will be interested in more than just your product/ service, price and ability to deliver. They'll want to know who they are working with on a day-to-day basis: who the key contacts are, who is the person for escalation of issues should problems arise that are not resolved to their liking etc. While they will certainly need to build an immediate rapport with *you* (assuming you are the first representative of your business that they come into contact with), and they will need to like you to want to work with you, that won't be enough. Buyers get fired for making bad decisions, so the individual who makes a decision to work with you not only has the best interests of the retailer, their employer, at heart but also needs to be sure that they are not taking any risks with their own career or credibility either.

As mentioned before, the key to this is surrounding yourself with the right people. Those people will supplement your skills and expertise, plug any gaps you may have, and add gravitas to your organization. I've got a couple of examples to bring this to life.

CASE STUDY   Client A

I've worked with a few clients who have presented to Angels Den, Europe's largest network of independent business investors, for investment. In their pre-pitch coaching they talk about the four things investors want to see from a business – product, passion, people and payback. I think it would be obvious to most people that an investor would need to know about payback and would want to understand the product. It's also not too much of a surprise that they'd want to see passion – after all, a business owner without passion for their business really ought to reconsider what they are doing! What comes as a surprise to many of the business owners who approach Angels Den is how important investors consider the team around you to be. They don't expect them to be employees; they just want to know that your skills/knowledge/expertise as a business owner are well supported by a credible group of others. Angels Den told one of my clients that he only had three out of four of the critical ingredients for success, and told him to come back to them when he could demonstrate he had plugged his own knowledge/skills gaps with the right team of people. That's how I met him – he needed to add a retail expert to his team and he chose me. Next time he presented to Angels Den he had a total of eight people included on his business plan – I was one of them – and he was accepted into the next stage, delivering his pitch to potential investors.

A retail buyer will also be keen to understand more about the key individuals in your business: in the same way it gives investors greater confidence that you'll be able to deliver your business plan, it gives retailers greater confidence that you're a credible business, with people who can deliver on the promises you make.

CASE STUDY   Client B

Another client of mine had developed an innovative marketing solution for retailers. The founders are two young entrepreneurial guys in their late 20s. They had the passion, the vision, they saw a gap in the market and thus had the product, but they had *no* expertise in retail and *no* past track record in the area they'd developed. They knew that to look credible in a pitch to a potential retail client they needed to give their team a boost. They did this by engaging several people either as non-executive directors or on a consultancy/freelance basis to bolster their knowledge and increase their gravitas. I worked with them to help them develop their go-to-market strategy – to ensure that they were 'talking the right language' to the retailers. One of the non-executive directors was very well known and well respected in the industry they were entering, so he was able to facilitate introductions (and with his reputation he was able to open doors for my client that would otherwise have proved almost impossible to achieve). Each of the people they'd introduced to the business had a valuable contribution to make and thus they had a greater level of success.

By surrounding themselves with this team of expert advisers they looked bigger than they actually were. They also looked credible, worth paying attention to. They were able to secure meetings with some significant retailers as a direct result of the team surrounding them and then, owing to the preparation I'd done with them, the business owners (the ones full of passion and with the most detailed product knowledge) were able to deliver their pitch confidently to the retailers, securing several lucrative contracts.

So, as you can see from the two case studies, there is no doubt that to sell successfully to retailers, even to get a foot in the door or to sound credible in a meeting, can depend on being surrounded by the right people.

Consider these questions for your business:

- What skills/knowledge gaps do you have?
- Where are you lacking in sector expertise?
- Who would you ideally include in your business if you could get them on board?

If you secure the support of the best third parties that you can afford, it will go a long way to making your business look more credible, worthy of more than a passing glance, and a safer option in the eyes of a retail buyer.

That's all very well and good, but as touched on above in my case study for client B, it was the business owner who initiated and managed the relationship with the retail client and ideally it will be *you* who should go in front of your potential clients. Why? Well, as with client B, you'll:

- have the passion;
- know more about your product than anyone else;
- be more deeply connected to your business vision;
- be the one who can make a call in a negotiation as you'll understand the importance of each client and will also know about the financials better than anyone you might delegate to in the early days.

So, because of this, in the early days you need to be the face of your business, driving forward the client relationships and being the main salesperson.

Considering that it's *you* that the retailer ultimately needs to believe in, have a meeting with, negotiate with, you need to make sure that you look as credible as possible. That leads us into your professional profile.

Importance of your profile

Now you are the figurehead of your business you have to think about everything you say, do and present about yourself that is in the public domain – from conversations with your friends on Facebook to your online profiles. You have to imagine 'what if my next big client opportunity saw this – what would they think of me?'; 'could what I am about to do/say damage my future business opportunities?' We live in an online, social, connected world and while these things can be leveraged to enormous advantage, unfortunately – and remembering the Second World War poster 'Careless talk costs lives' – misuse of publicly visible content can have a negative impact and cost business relationships.

It's worth investing some time in writing your profile to position yourself as the business owner/expert/innovator. You will need this content for online sites (your own and others) as well as for any press/media enquiries you get.

If you are unsure about how to write it, take a look at professional profiles for business people you admire and aspire to be like. Look at the way they present themselves, the style of language and the content they use. Can you replicate the style/format but with your own unique content? Think about what you can say about yourself that will resonate with others, that will engender trust and that will make them feel confident about connecting with you and potentially doing business with you.

Once you've created your profile you need to check it relatively frequently – I'd suggest at least quarterly – to make sure that it's still relevant and still how you want to be 'known' to others – customers, suppliers, colleagues and the outside world.

Your profile should be visible in all relevant media – the simplest way to publish your profile is online, so we'll look at that now.

Using online tools to leverage your profile and your expertise

There are so many social networks and online tools where you can include your professional profile, we're not going to look at them all. I want to focus on the most important ones: LinkedIn, Facebook, YouTube, Twitter, your own website and a blog. I'm not planning to teach you how to use them (there's plenty of online help and advice for that, often freely available), but I will explain how you can leverage these online tools and media to enable you to establish your professional credibility, to be well referenced online, and to ensure you're leaving the right lasting impression should a retail buyer do some research to find out a bit more about you.

Figure 3.1 on pages 60–62 reviews the most popular online media available, how it is positioned/what it is for, and what you can/cannot include by way of profile content. It will give you an idea about the options available to you. You need to decide what's best for you – although I'd really urge you to get on LinkedIn, if you are not already, as you'll be able to connect with people who will either be within your ideal buyer's organization or able to help you get a foot in the door.

We need to consider *why* each of the elements in the table is important to you, to your profile and for your credibility. Looking at aspects of Figure 3.1, let's explore that further:

- **Profile text**: This text will often be the first 'contact' someone has with you – so it needs to give them a great first impression. You need to consider how you position your profile to be relevant and attractive to the right audience, including key information that puts you in the best possible light, removing information that is irrelevant.

  You also need to consider the 'tone of voice' – you need to make sure that you're using the right style, not only for the content, but also the way it is written, as this will have an impact on how the reader perceives you.

  Essentially it's not only what you say, but how you say it!

- **Profile image**: As a business person you need to have a professional-looking image, ideally from a professional photographer who does head-shots for business people. If you notice the profiles on social networks that have amateur images, snaps, or something a bit 'silly', what does that make you think about the person? However, Facebook is a bit different – your personal profile can be social, but don't lose sight of the fact that your content *will* be in the public eye, searchable and visible, so if you want to be taken seriously you need to moderate *all* online content (as I will explore further below), and your image is part of this.

FIGURE 3.1 How to use online sites to enhance your professional profile

Media	Style	Profile text	Image	Recommendations	Content distribution	Links
LinkedIn	Professional online network. Mainly employees of larger businesses and freelance professionals.	Substantial space available. Includes professional headline, summary and expertise as well as a comprehensive past career history.	A singe profile image is allowed.	Recommendations can only be requested by each 'job' you've had in the past, not for the profile holder generically. You must be connected to an individual within LinkedIn in order for them to be able to recommend you.	Status updates enable you to share content and you can also post in groups. There are a variety of 'apps' allowing you to add a blog and other content.	Up to three links to your website/blog/ other pages can be added to your LinkedIn profile.
Facebook	Social, informal – you have the choice to use a personal profile or a page (representing you as a business persons or your brand) – however, you must have a personal profile in order to create a page.	Whether using Facebook as a page or as your own profile there is plenty of space for profile text, similar to LinkedIn.	Each profile/ page has a main image and other images can be associated.	Recommendations are not structured. People can 'Like' a page and this acts as loose endorsement, but doesn't carry as much weight as the clear recommendation content on LinkedIn.	Status updates, 'shares' and 'likes' are all forms of content distribution enabled by Facebook.	You can have a link to your preferred webpage from your profile and from your page info.

FIGURE 3.1 *continued*

Media	Style	Profile text	Image	Recommendations	Content distribution	Links
YouTube	YouTube is primarily a platform for sharing video content. While there is some discussion connected to the content, in the main, users simply host content on YouTube, which then allows it to be shared elsewhere.	The ideal scenario is for a business owner (or brand) to have a YouTube 'channel' which can be customized to include profile text and also aligned to brand colours.	A channel can include an image or logo as it's 'identifier'.	Those viewing your video content can 'like', 'favourite' or 'share' it. If your settings allow it, users can also embed your video into their own online content. These actions are similar to, but not the same as, a recommendation.	YouTube is designed specifically to allow the distribution of video content.	You can have a link on your channel.
Twitter	This is a short, snappy mode of communication, a mix of content, from broadcasting brand messages to conversations and content sharing.	Very short headline – only 160 characters.	An image, known as your 'avatar', is allowed.	Inferred by the number of followers, or by the 'retweeting' of your content. No specific recommendations are enabled.	Short messages, links, images and videos – all contained within 140 characters.	You can include a link to your preferred landing page within your profile content.

FIGURE 3.1 *continued*

Media	Style	Profile text	Image	Recommendations	Content distribution	Links
Company website	As discussed in Chapters 1 and 2, a website is necessary and should be in keeping with your business identity and presence.	As much as you feel fits with the content/focus of the site. Usually the founder/owner profile is part of the general 'about us' content or a 'meet the team' page.	As this is your website you have greater flexibility over how many images you choose to share.	You can include a page of testimonials – this may be more specific to the product/service and less about the individual. Testimonials on your own website are not as compelling as those on a third-party site as there is always the possibility that an unscrupulous person may fabricate recommendations!	You can obviously share content from your site via all of the social media, as well as ensure it is indexed in search and referenced in outbound e-mails.	You can elect to include links to any content on other sites as you see fit.
Blog	A tool for you to platform your knowledge, expertise, opinions, thoughts and ideas. Great for demonstrating how, as the business owner, you are knowledgeable and up to speed with relevant issues. If you are a good writer, a blog is an essential marketing tool for your business.	A full profile can be included on a blog.	Your professional image can appear on the primary blogger profile. The blog can carry your branding and look similar to your website. Each article can include images.	Readers can 'like' posts and share posts on their own social media, which is an implied endorsement. Readers can additionally add comments to posts, which infer endorsement. However, there is no ability to seek recommendations for the writer.	Blog tools have various in-built sharing capabilities that can automatically share content on to linked social media. It can also be manually shared. Readers can subscribe to a blog via e-mail or RSS.	A 'blog-roll' enables you to create a list of links. You can also include links in your profile text, pages and posts. It is very flexible.

- **Recommendations**: This is a very powerful way to back up all the claims you make about yourself and your expertise in both your profile text and through the content you share. If you can generate positive comment and recommendations from others, it will be more compelling to a reader than anything you can say about yourself. Think about this in your own experience – you're more likely to make a judgement about buying a holiday, a car or a product if the information provided by the seller is not only good but is backed up by '5 star' past-customer reviews. The same is true for judging people. I know from my own experience that if someone has invited me to connect on social media and I discover that they are connected to several people whom I consider credible, I will connect to them more readily, even if I don't know them personally.

  There is also something I've called the 'chain of credibility'. You could consider this when it comes to requesting recommendations. Earlier I suggested using LinkedIn as your primary tool to establish your expertise *and* to connect to the right individuals in retail organizations. Another benefit of LinkedIn is that when you are connected to someone you can ask them to give you a recommendation. I've found that the seniority or credibility of the person recommending you reflects on you. Equally, if you notice that someone is recommended by someone who in turn is highly recommended, there is a sense of 'wow, that person must be good if someone like that recommended them' – this is what I mean by chain of credibility. Any recommendation is good for you, but if you can get a couple of really high-quality ones, from highly regarded people, that will stand you out from the crowd.

- **Content you share**: While much of what you share, and how you share it, depends on the media you are using, you must still consider the impression it will give a reader. There are some general rules that seem to work well. Essentially the recommendations from experts in the field suggest you should:

1 Share the content of others. You should share content that is relevant to, or connected with, your main area of expertise. This will demonstrate that you distribute material that people interested in similar things to you might want to read. The purpose is to highlight that you are someone 'on the ball' with topical issues.

2 Comment on the content of others. Try to add an opinion, thought or perspective on the content published by others that is relevant to, or connected with, your core area of expertise. It engages you in a conversation with them and it also demonstrates a bit of personality – you're not backward at coming forward! Comments on news articles and well-read blogs are also a great way for you to get noticed.

3 Generate original content. Share your own thoughts, ideas, opinions and perspectives – promote your knowledge and expertise, share some of what you are about and make it easier for people to understand more about you as a business person. This can include blogs, videos, web pages etc. Accepted good practice advises that you don't only focus on 'selling' messages but additionally on something of relevant interest, for example, why you are passionate about your product/service, what inspired you to create it. Online content is more interesting to a reader when it is connected to a persona and not just a remote, 'faceless' brand/product.

As with all publicly visible information you must ensure you're sharing the right kind of things – do some 'mental filtering' before putting anything into the public domain. Think how that content would reflect on you; how it would influence a retail buyer, if they read it.

- **Links:** These are important for your search marketing. Inbound links to your website increase its importance in the eyes of search engines – it's called off-site SEO or link-building by search marketers. Any links that point at your website are beneficial to you. I won't give you a lesson in off-site SEO, but if you want to know more about this you will find plenty of content about the value of inbound links if you do an online search.

I hope that explains a bit more as to why all of these types of profile content are important to you, to your business, and in positioning you as an expert in your field. These are all key ingredients for ensuring you come across as a credible professional when engaging in conversations with retailers.

Next we're going to look at stepping that up a gear and leveraging all this fantastic content about you, not only to position you as an expert but to make you *the* expert in your niche.

Being the go-to expert in your niche

Making proactive contact with your ideal audience, knocking on doors and phoning up for meetings is one way to increase your sales. Having customers come to you is another way. I bet you can guess which one is easier... obviously the latter! In an ideal world we want to create your brand, expertise, product, service – whatever you've got – as *the* one that everyone wants. We want to create loads of positive PR, media coverage, online content, third-party endorsement etc about you so that retail buyers hear about what you've got to offer and approach you directly. Much of what follows in the subsequent chapters of this book will contribute to that, as we look at how every success you have can be turned into positive conversations about your brand that make you increasingly well known and increasingly attractive to others.

In order that you can identify those opportunities to create some 'noise' about your business, expertise and success, I'm going to give you a list of things you should be trying to generate for you and your business *right now*:

- **Press coverage:** Have you got a story to tell about you, your business or your customers that would be interesting as a feature for their readership?

- Press like stories that resonate with readers. If you can explain your business journey, inspiration, challenges and lessons learnt, you can potentially get articles out in publications. Make sure you focus on the ones that your ideal customers would be reading, of course. You don't need to be overly promotional, in fact if it's an interesting story you'll pique the interest of the reader and they'll come to you – this is part of the process of becoming a go-to expert; interested parties contact you.

- **Regular press feature:** Could you offer to write a regular feature that would be a value-add to the readership and make the editor's job easier?

  - Linked to the above, once you've developed a relationship with an editor or journalist you can offer to provide a regular feature, which means that readers will see you repeatedly. From that repetition, in a publication they read and trust, they will come to trust you and remember you. This means that should they have the need for what you offer at some future date they will think of you first of all.

- **Case studies:** Can you describe a customer success and include that on your website and on other online content? Can the customer press-release the case study/success story so it gets picked up by the press?

  - If you can get a success story written up, and mainly focused on what a customer has been able to achieve thanks to you, then this is a further, compelling, third-party recommendation that brings to life the value-add that your product or services can bring to a customer. It could be as simple as a boutique retailer talking about how, by adding your product to their range, they've been able to increase sales as it's exactly what their customers want. The key is that the case study comes from the customer, including a quote from you and references to your business, but essentially the power of something like this is again the fact that an independent third party is willing to endorse the claims you make about your business.

- **Guest blogging**: Can you contribute valuable insights, lessons learnt, hints and tips to a well-read blog?

  - Similar to providing an article to press, often blogs have high readership and are, in essence, a form of online press. Getting a feature as a guest blogger is as beneficial to you as getting a feature in the press, so long as the blog is reaching the right audience for you.

- **Guest speaking**: Can you present about a case study, success story or similar to an audience at any specific events?

  - Event organizers are often looking for interesting speakers. If you can leverage your press coverage/guest blogging and case studies to demonstrate what you could talk about to share your expertise, lessons learnt etc with an audience, you may find it is a great way to generate more interest in you and your business. The key is to be selective – only events with some relevance to your ideal audience would be worth giving up your time for. Think about the trade shows and exhibitions that include keynote content – see if there is a way that you can put yourself forward to give a useful presentation to the audience while at the same time making connections with people who may potentially be your ideal customer.

- **Media coverage**: You can contact the news desk of local TV and radio to introduce yourself as a business owner/expert, able to comment on any news relating to your specific topic. If news breaks, call them up and suggest that you can comment on a story for them.

  - If you can get yourself on the 'preferred list' of a news desk for the local TV or radio channel it means that you'll be called upon as and when a feature potentially relevant to your expertise comes up – of course, you're helping them out too, so as long as you deliver what they're looking for you'll stay on the preferred list!

- **Write a book:** There is no doubt, and I speak from personal experience, that if you can get a publisher to produce your book you will have lasting evidence of your expertise!

  - To most people the idea of writing a book is impossible, abhorrent, something that would never even cross their mind. It's very likely that your ideal customer would think this too. Just imagine what they'll think of you if you are a published author and can give them a gift of a signed copy of your book! It's certainly going to make you stand out from the crowd! It may take you some time to figure out what your 'story' would be, but keep this in mind as it might be something to consider in the future.

The purpose of all of this is to ensure that you, and therefore your business, are positioned as the go-to brand for the niche you serve. By focusing on the niche and the expertise in the business, you divert attention away from the actual size of the business and become the *only* credible contender that a customer might want to do business with. Of course, there is a fine balance between being seen as the figurehead for your business and being seen as the primary resource in the business. This is a key part of how to look big – *not* allowing yourself to be seen as the only person in the business, the one who does everything. It's very easy to confuse your expert, figurehead positioning with being the person who does everything. You need to make it very clear that while you lead the business, shape its vision, purpose and direction, your business itself delivers its proposition through an extended team (some in-house, some outsourced). This is fundamental to presenting a congruent, believable proposition to potential buyers – *you* are seen as a thought-leader, driving a scalable business forward. Your business is able to deliver a niche proposition *and* to support a high level of demand should a major retailer want to place a big order with you. You and the business are obviously connected, but the business is not you alone.

As we've just established that it's not going to be you all on your own, a wider network of people need to come into the picture. Before we complete this chapter, let's look at your extended team.

The extended team

You may not immediately decide to employ a team, favouring out-sourcing or using contractors. Whichever model suits you in terms of pulling the team together, in order to look big you need to give the impression of being surrounded by, and supported by, the right kind of people. As I explained earlier, when talking about the clients presenting at Angels Den, this isn't just about the selling/delivery side of things – if you are going to seek investment finance or bank finance they too will want to know how you are structured and resourced in order to support your growth.

It may sound a bit daunting at first but I have a simple example approach that you might want to follow in order to plan for what you need to have in place. Obviously your business may have some specifics that add additional steps to this simplified approach, but broadly speaking I am sure you'll get the idea!

1 Outline all the business activities that need to happen to deliver your service proposition – think about the overall process and all the 'back office' support functions.

2 Determine what skills/capabilities enable your business to undertake those actions – determine how elements of processes can be grouped and responsibility for delivering whole chunks of process can be assigned to an outsourcer or an employee.

3 Identify the partners/people who have those skills and capabilities – decide what is core to the business; what *must* be done in-house versus what could be outsourced. Then research options – who can you approach who may be a great outsource partner? Who can you think of that you'd want in your business as an employee/contractor?

4 Make contact with those people/partners to find out if they are interested in working with your business, and if so, what terms they would consider working with you on. You can be quite creative, offering things like equity shares in lieu of salary etc to people who would be an asset to the business. Make sure

you do your research (online) about the people and partners you engage – you want them to align to your culture, values and ethics and to really back up your credibility with your ideal customer.

When you have the right partners and people in your business it enables you to make commitments to customers confidently, and it enables potential customers to make commitments, confidently, to buy from you.

Wrapping up

In this chapter we considered your people, focusing on how leveraging your own profile and expertise, as well as that of others around you in business, makes your business look big and positions you as the go-to brand for the niche you serve.

We have covered how to:

- give the impression of calibre and capability;
- leverage third-party review to stand out as 'thought-leaders' or innovators;
- focus on your niche and expertise, diverting attention away from size;
- balance being seen as an expert/figurehead without looking like the only resource;
- make use of a 'virtual team' to add substance without the heavy overhead/commitment of employment.

That concludes this chapter, the last in Part One: Look Big.

Part One: Look Big – summing up

You now know how important it is to look big if you want to sell successfully to retailers. I can't reiterate enough how cautious retailers can be about who they do business with – big companies feel safer buying from big companies.

In this part of the book we have focused on the impression/impact that your business makes, so that if a retail buyer was considering working with you there would be no aspects of your business that gave them cause for concern or made them feel that perhaps it was just a bit too risky to work with a smaller business. We've invested a lot of time and energy in ensuring that the question about the size of your business doesn't even enter their heads.

This part has been centred on the aim to 'punch above your weight' – I've used the saying 'dress for the job you want, not the job you've got' and I hope that's what we've done with the business – dressed it for the client it wants, not the clients it can easily get.

So the three chapters in this part have reviewed:

1 business identity;

2 business presence;

3 people.

There are key areas to focus on from each chapter that are the critical ingredients you should have in place when it comes to looking big. With that in mind, we'll wrap up this part with a simple checklist (Figure 3.2) for you to go through to make sure that you've got all the ingredients in place to be looking big and really punching above your weight. Each area is listed – you need to ask yourself honestly if that area has been completed to your satisfaction or if there is still work to be done. If you answer yes, there are likely to be no actions (other than to keep it up). If you answer no, you should summarize the actions you need to put in place to ensure you're able to project the right image and to avoid any doubts forming in the mind of a retail buyer that might stop them from doing business with you.

This checklist is also available for download, if you prefer, via **www.retailchampion.co.uk/selling-to-retailers/resources**.

continued on page 74

FIGURE 3.2   Part One checklist

Area	Ingredient	Complete? (yes/no)	Action to address (if any)	Cost implications?	Priority (H/M/L)	Target date to complete
Identity	Defining your mission and positioning					
Identity	Considering what your culture, ethics and values are					
Identity	Developing your branding/visual identity					
Presence	Confirming your business name, address, phone					
Presence	Creating your marketing materials – business cards, brochure, 'leave-behind' materials					
Presence	Securing your web domains, e-mail address and the website itself					

Presence	Scoping out your search marketing strategy and plans			
Presence	Deciding on your social media strategy and plans			
People	Developing your profile as the business owner – how it is written to position you as a credible, recommended, trusted, go-to expert			
People	Checking your individual online presence – ensuring it is consistent, congruent, creating the right impression, using relevant media			
People	Bolstering the business with experts – the extended team			

Part One: Look Big – summing up   *continued*

Now you've completed the checklist, the onus is on you to actually implement the actions to address the gaps. This and all subsequent checklists include columns for you to estimate the cost implications, prioritize the actions and assign a due date. The intent is for you to create a plan that is realistic and one you can act on, not just an exercise in paperwork, so please do take the planned actions forward.

Having successfully completed Part One we're ready to move on to Part Two: Plan Big. This part will include three chapters: Customer, Competition and Scalability.

PART TWO
Plan Big

In Part One we invested considerable effort in making sure that your business looks robust, credible and worthy of trust from a potential retail client. This part is all about making sure you've done the groundwork to live up to that impression. Remember my positioning mantra? Well, by implementing all of the aspects of 'looking big' you have made or implied explicit promises about your brand and capabilities. You need now to be in a position to live up to those promises or you will risk losing any credibility you have created.

In this part we'll be looking at what you need to know about your market – the customer and the competition – as well as how you intend to scale up to serve your customer. The outcome should be clarity, based on detailed research and analysis, about whom to approach, what your points of difference are if compared to the competition, and how you can guarantee a reliable and consistent supply of goods (or services) to your customer should they place their business with you.

Through the next three chapters we will be looking at the areas of:

1 your ideal or target customer (mindful of both the end consumer and the retail buyer);

2 your competition – who they are, what they offer, how you differentiate (leveraging your positioning);

3 your ability to deliver – how you can scale to the demands of a major client (leveraging your people).

Once again, at the end of this part we'll do a recap on the key components of 'Plan Big', with a Part Two checklist for you to go through to make sure you've got all the necessary ingredients in place.

Customer

04

Introduction

In this chapter, the first of Part Two on Plan Big, we'll be focusing on a very important group in more detail – your customer. Clearly the ability to recognize and serve your customer is the most critical aspect of your business – you owe your existence to them – so this chapter will be pivotal to all the chapters that follow. Make sure you spend an appropriate amount of time clarifying your own under-standing about the key attributes of your customer and what drives them to buy from you (or buy your product from retailers).

So, in order to achieve this we'll be:

- looking at how you can identify an ideal customer, considering the differences between the buyer (the person who makes the decision to procure your goods/services, the person who signs off your invoices) and the end user (the person who the product or service is 'for');

- using a couple of case studies to illustrate the importance of really understanding the customer from two different perspectives – Neil Westwood from Magic Whiteboard and Emma Wimhurst from Diva Cosmetics;

- discussing how major retailers are more likely to be interested in buying into your product or services if you've already proven demand for it;

- considering ways to seek out and connect with the right people to approach in retail organizations, what they are likely to be motivated by, and what their objectives are;

- talking about your pricing. Pricing is part of the positioning we talked about in Chapter 1. Understanding how to define your pricing is key to ensuring you present a great-value proposition to your customer *and* make a profit.

Defining your ideal customer

If you develop products for consumers, the chances are you have a pretty clear idea who your ideal customer is – you'll have had them in mind when creating the product. It should be fairly easy for you (if you are a product supplier) to develop your detailed ideal customer description. In your case, the retailer is the conduit through which you can reach your ideal customer, a distribution channel, possibly one of several if you also sell direct via e-commerce for instance (we'll consider that in a bit more detail later in this chapter). As a product supplier, knowing your ideal end user makes it considerably easier to identify your retail customer – because you can review the market and determine which retailers would typically attract your ideal customer.

If you are selling services to a retailer then your ideal customer, the end user, may not necessarily be the consumer. That said, in many cases services suppliers are still very much intending that their output is used by, or is an influence on, the consumer. Think about service providers such as e-commerce website designers, in-store merchandising fixture manufacturers, point of sale printers or payment processing solutions – all of these services are purchased by the retailer but the end user, the person who is impacted by them, is the consumer. The subtle difference in this scenario is that the service provider will almost always have the ability to tailor their offer to suit the retailer, in order that when it is implemented it is well suited to that specific retailer's customer base. With product suppliers this approach, tailoring the product uniquely to align to the retailers' customer base, is less common – but it is what Emma Wimhurst did with Diva Cosmetics and it is a very smart approach. We'll be looking at Emma's case study in more detail later in this chapter.

For many who develop services it may well be that someone else in the retail organization (not your buyer) is the end user. Think of software, for instance: the buyer is usually a person in an IT department and the end user is someone within the organization whose job is made easier, more efficient, or better, as a result of the purchase and implementation of the software. Of course, the consumer still benefits when a retailer is more efficient or more profitable as this means that the retail brand can grow, present a better offer, deliver better service to the consumer etc. In my earlier career I was often involved in software selection, choosing tools that would enable the retail business processes and systems to become more robust and repeatable, creating a more scalable business platformed for growth, thus adding value to the organization. One aspect we always considered in software selection was 'how does this internal improvement benefit our customer?' Successful retailers *always* have an eye on the customer impact of their business decisions, whether it is a direct or indirect impact. They consider everything, from the ethical and environmental impacts (if they make bad choices it may alienate their customers, while good choices could lead to positive press coverage) through to profitability and service-level impacts (bearing in mind that big companies have their shareholders/investors to consider as well as the consumer, so being more profitable and offering better service would be key factors). So something that anyone selling to a retailer should bear in mind is not only to consider what's in it for the buyer but also how the offer, product or service, can positively impact, directly or indirectly, the customer experience and the bottom-line profitability.

Your ideal customer

Now it's time to use your imagination a bit. I want you to actually visualize your ideal customer, not as a generic group but as an individual. Create a mental picture of the customer and then begin to make some notes to describe them in real detail. This is your 'pen-portrait' of your customer.

It may initially be counterintuitive to focus on just one individual, but of course there are many customers sufficiently similar to your ideal customer to ensure you have a wide enough market to sell to, and in volumes that will deliver profitability. There are benefits to defining clearly your ideal customer; for instance, it's much easier to write compelling marketing copy when you have an individual in mind that you are writing it for. Plus, if you ever find yourself in a situation with a retailer where it just doesn't seem to work, the relationship doesn't feel right, then the chances are that this isn't an ideal customer. It doesn't mean you can't sell to them, but it may mean the relationship isn't as solid as it would be if you were dealing with an ideal customer.

Below is an example of the level of detail you could go into; the reason for doing this is so that you can really develop a 'feeling' for how your customer would act/react in any given situation, and therefore how you can influence them.

Example ideal customer, product end user – pen-portrait

This ideal customer is one I've invented, by way of example, for a business I've done some work with. The business I have in mind has developed a range of healthy children's ready-meals. This ideal customer is their end user, not the retail buyer:

> Fiona is a 38-year-old full-time working mother of two children aged 9 months and 3 years. She is married to John, 43, who is an accountant. They live in a large detached house in Berkshire. Fiona has recently returned to her hectic job – she works in a London hospital as a registrar. Well paid, health conscious, and eager to provide the very best start in life to her children, Fiona spends the little spare time she has at weekends preparing and freezing home-cooked food that her au pair (who isn't a great cook) can defrost and give to the kids during the week. With her and John both commuting to London they are out of the house for at least 12 hours per day. Their weekends are very precious. They have limited family time but are comfortable financially.

Fiona is ideal for the healthy children's ready-meals – she completely understands the benefits of having good nutrition for her family, she already tries hard to achieve this in her limited free time. She is time poor and yet financially quite well off. I could continue my pen-portrait describing family holidays, the car they drive, the TV shows they watch, what publications they read, how and where they socialize... you get the idea? I am sure you could also continue the creation of Fiona's 'imaginary' life.

By going through this process and by visualizing your specific end customer as a person, someone you know so well they're as familiar to you as a friend, you'll have a far better understanding of what price point they will find acceptable, where they shop, how they shop etc. I often call this process 'creating your imaginary friend' – the person doesn't necessarily exist but if you get this right you can talk about your ideal customer in your business, with your team, and they will know where you are coming from. If your ideal customer was known as 'Sally', this could be a scenario in your office: 'We've got some new product ideas – I'm not sure about this one, I really don't see that "Sally" would buy this – what do you all think?' Of course the team know Sally, she's your ideal customer, and because she's been so well described they also understand her and can almost predict her decisions. They can let you know what they think; if it would or would not be a product that Sally would like. In this way you can validate decisions about product development, or indeed about which retailers to target, by asking yourself 'is this right for [name of ideal customer]?' It is a really powerful sense-check for you to make and it will ensure your business is making decisions that are customer-centric and not just based on what you or your team like, or what might be the easier, lower-cost option.

It works for services too – here's an example just to prove the point.

Example ideal customer, services end user – pen-portrait

Alan is the retail operations director for a major shoe shop chain with over 200 outlets. He is keen for his store managers to respond to local competition, local trends and other local market factors, by implementing store-specific promotions and in-store events. He is keen that his store managers are empowered to operate within an agreed framework to develop and then publicize these local promotions. He is keen for the store managers to have the ability to create store-specific window posters, based on a template with editable content, which can be printed in-store to save on cost. This will enable each store to have a unique focus as they know their local community best. Alan is researching options for a services provider who can help him to bring this capability to his managers. He is interested in quality, flexibility, ease of use and, of course, cost, but he wants to work with a supplier who will enable him to meet his objectives, to make him look good in the eyes of his boss, and to help him bring this new capability to his management team. Alan cares about what his colleagues think of him; he's been in the business nearly 20 years, having himself worked his way up through the organization from the shop floor. He knows the role of a store manager inside out and is well liked. He cares about the customer experience too, so he is eager to work with a supplier who is not only able to deliver the requirements but who also has a similar passion for enabling his business to achieve its objectives as he has.

As this is a business purchase it's not as 'personal' as the pen-portrait of Fiona in the first example, but you can still get a feel for Alan. Alan is the buyer, the store manager is the end user that he is buying for. The 'process' he is aiming to improve in the business is all about influencing and engaging the consumer – so as I touched on above, when Alan presents a business case to his boss he would be highly likely to reference 'impact on the customer' of the project he has in mind as well as all the other financial factors (costs and benefits) which would need to be included to justify the expenditure. With Alan as your ideal customer you'd probably need to ensure, when it came to selling to him, that you had a really good understanding of his business and of its customer. When Alan is your ideal customer it's clear that you should also invest time in building a strong, trust-based relationship as this will make a difference to him. Alan will need to believe that you are a supplier that he can trust to protect his reputation with the rest of the team and to help him to deliver on his objectives. Focusing on finding buyers like Alan will mean you can develop an effective selling style that will really resonate with people like him. If you know that culturally this kind of customer is a great fit for your business, it is likely that you will develop long-term, quality supplier–customer relationships. It doesn't mean you won't sell to non-ideal customers, but you must be mindful that some customers are a better 'fit' for the way you do business and others are less well aligned to your culture and values. You'll probably enjoy working with those who are more ideal, while finding it more challenging, less enjoyable, to work with those who are not ideal.

So, before we move on, please take some time to consider who is your ideal customer. I'd like you to take the time to make some notes so that you can develop this 'pen-portrait' and eventually leverage this within your business. The picture can evolve over time and as your business matures (especially if you are relatively recently established). It will inevitably develop, becoming clearer and more refined as you work it through and reflect on it. Eventually it will become second nature; you'll wonder how you ever made decisions without first considering your ideal customer.

Knowing your customer – case studies

There are different approaches to customer understanding, and before moving on to the next section of this chapter I will illustrate these using a couple of case studies. In writing this book I had the pleasure of interviewing two fantastic entrepreneurs who have successfully sold to retailers.

The case studies are Magic Whiteboard and Diva Cosmetics. They are both product suppliers but the Diva Cosmetics approach is less about the actual product and more about the end-to-end service proposition.

CASE STUDY 1 Magic Whiteboard – a product created specifically with an end user in mind

Neil Westwood, founder of Magic Whiteboard, was working as an NHS trainer; his area of expertise was lean thinking. When he had to deliver training it always involved taking lots of heavy, cumbersome equipment, such as a whiteboard, to a hospital ward. It was impractical and he needed an easier, more portable, solution. He decided to develop Magic Whiteboard to make his life easier, developing a lightweight, portable alternative to a rigid whiteboard. His solution was whiteboard material, on a roll, which could be stuck to any flat surface on a temporary basis (with no damage to the surface), and then packed away again at the end of a training session.

Neil initially had in mind that this solution would be great for him and all the other trainers who had to travel to various locations to deliver their training. He understood his market and his customer – essentially it was 'people like him'. He set to work and found a manufacturer and from there on he developed the product that is now retailed through various office supplies outlets as Magic Whiteboard (and associated additional items that have since been developed).

In the beginning Neil didn't plan to sell to retail; he was focused on selling to more people like him. Initially he developed an e-commerce platform through which he was able to sell to other training providers. To increase his reach he visited trade shows where he was also able to sell direct to trainers. In the early days Neil really knew and understood the end user – people just like him. He didn't need to do too much research into his customer either – he had the benefit of the ultimate understanding of his customer, as he'd developed a product *he* needed.

About 18 months after he launched Magic Whiteboard Neil's friends encouraged him to apply to go on the TV show *Dragon's Den*. On the show entrepreneurs and inventors present their products to well-known investors with the aim of securing their support and financing to take their business forward. He thought it would be great exposure, a great opportunity for him to increase his reach, to be seen on national TV, whether he got investment or not, so he applied. His plan, should he be successful in securing a 'Dragon' investor, was to use their investment to take Magic Whiteboard forward. At this point he still saw it as a product for trainers and was not considering the retail opportunity.

Neil was successful on *Dragon's Den* – I actually remember seeing him on the show! He secured two investors – Deborah Meaden and Theo Paphitis. Deborah is known for her PR and marketing prowess, Theo is the owner of retail businesses. One of Theo's retail brands is Ryman – a high-street office products chain. Of course, Theo immediately saw the potential to take the Magic Whiteboard to retailers and to expand the customer base enormously. It was a winning combination – Theo had all the connections and the retail-know-how, Deborah could turbo-charge the PR and marketing, and Neil had a really deep understanding of how the end user could benefit from the product.

So in this example the product was created entirely with an end user in mind and retail became an opportune channel to market, to widen the reach of a product that had already proven its value to the training sector. One of the key aspects of Neil's success was his absolute belief in the product (as an end user himself) and the evidence of an engaged audience as a result of his existing customer base.

CASE STUDY 2   Diva Cosmetics – a service, solution and product tailored for the retailer

Emma Wimhurst created Diva Cosmetics to address a gap in the market. She had many years of expertise working in the branded cosmetics industry and she noticed that fashion retailers didn't typically offer a fashion colour cosmetics assortment. She felt they were missing an opportunity to make incremental sales and margin. She decided to do something about it.

Emma always expected to sell to retailers; she never had any direct selling strategy, as at the time that she was starting up the internet was still very new so e-commerce/online selling was not a viable option. Other channels would have been too slow (catalogue sales etc) and would have required her to have a wholly different business model, holding stock of her items and investing heavily in a sales campaign. So, for Emma, her only focus was to sell to retail right from the outset.

Her approach was different from that of a 'typical' product supplier – while Emma intended to supply products, her approach was much more like a services supplier. She intended to design and develop a range of products uniquely for each of her retailer customers. Essentially Diva Cosmetics was not only a product supplier but a whole outsourced category management team, providing the retailer with everything it needed – consumer insights, research, product design and development, liaison with production, shipping and packaging, and the whole of the supply chain management process. Emma's business model saved her customers the trouble of creating and resourcing a new department to manage a colour cosmetics category. This was a brilliant proposition for her ideal customer, high-street fashion retailers, who had absolutely no experience in developing a cosmetics offering.

Emma's approach was to identify retailers that she believed had an opportunity to sell colour cosmetics, so she focused on fashion retailers with a high number of teenage customers who were influenced by popular culture. Emma's business launched at the time when the pop group The Spice Girls was hugely influential on teenage girls who wanted to express their own 'Girl Power' with vivid colours in both their clothing and make-up choices. So, leveraging her detailed knowledge of the consumer and the industry, Emma was able to present each retailer with a unique proposition, perfectly tailored to meet their customer expectations, aligned to their positioning, with appropriate product, pricing and presentation.

Emma's career prior to setting up Diva had given her all the market and product knowledge she needed, but it was the way she used her knowledge that secured her rapid growth and huge success, right from the start. Her relentless focus on fashion, trends, the market, colours, celebrity – all of which influenced the end user – made Diva a real hit with its retail clients.

Emma's approach was different from Neil's in that she targeted retailers she believed could sell a fashion cosmetics offer. She then delved into detail to understand who their customer base was in order to present product concepts that would be a real winner for each retailer uniquely. She turned the process of developing products for a customer on its head; instead of defining a market for a product, she defined a product for a market. That might be something you can do too.

Emma's brand is probably not one you have ever heard of – and that's because it wasn't about her brand, it was about her total service and solution, which included a product. Diva Cosmetics might not be a well-known consumer brand but it was behind the launch of fashion cosmetics into major high-street retailers such as New Look, River Island, Claire's Accessories and George at Asda – a client list I am sure most small businesses would be very proud to have.

So, whichever way you approach 'knowing the end customer', it's obviously imperative that you *do* know them. Of course, it's the buyer who signs the contract, the order and the invoice, so we'll explore them in more detail shortly. Just before that, I want to dig a little deeper into how to really prove the market, as Neil had done with Magic Whiteboard.

Reaching the end user

Often, to influence the actual buyer – the person who makes the purchasing decision – you need to demonstrate 'appetite' with your end users. If you're selling product, that can be relatively easy – you can add additional channels and sell direct as Neil did. If you are selling services that's a little more difficult, but not impossible!

Your options can include:

- selling direct, through e-commerce or other channels (more relevant for products);
- using social media to gauge opinion;
- doing structured market research and analysis to demonstrate size of market.

Figure 4.1 explores the pros and cons of each and when they could be best used.

FIGURE 4.1   Approaches to reach the end user

Method	Pros	Cons	When best used
E-commerce	You can provide detailed sales stats, conversion figures (ratio of number of visitors to number of transactions) and demonstrate that the consumer has appetite for the product at the given price.	Can be expensive to implement, and in order to drive sufficient traffic to it to deliver a decent sales rate you'll need to invest in the ongoing promotion of the site.	Not a one-off, this is a long-term, ongoing investment in a direct channel to market. You would not have e-commerce purely to prove your market; however, if you planned to have e-commerce anyway, it would help you to prove your market.
Social media	Instant, free to use, open – you'll potentially get a wide range of feedback quite swiftly.	Random – you can't control the audience giving feedback so it may not be representative of your ideal customer. You also need to have a sufficiently engaged audience on social media for them to bother to provide feedback.	Great if you have a strong following and you want to gauge opinion on ideas, concepts or thoughts. You may need an incentive to encourage people to take time to comment. It's a less formal approach; it can give you some indications of the market but should not be your only source of research.

FIGURE 4.1   *continued*

Method	Pros	Cons	When best used
Market research	Structured, focused, independent and will enable you to gain insights into the key questions/ concerns that matter most to you and to your potential retail buyer. It will provide a quality, relevant output if undertaken professionally.	You have to pay for a quality service, and it won't be cheap. It may take time to prepare the surveys or complete the analysis.	Any serious business ought to undertake some form of market research – it will be expected by investors, banks and buyers to demonstrate that you're a 'safe bet'. Ideally you should invest in research as well as trying out other options in parallel. Good research will deliver return on investment. It will ensure that in the early days you are focused on what is relevant and appropriate for the market, and ensure you're not 'barking up the wrong tree'.

As you will appreciate, anything you can do to demonstrate to your buyer that there is appetite for your product or service will go a long way to securing their trust in you when it comes to the pitch. With that in mind, let's now look at your ideal buyer in more detail to understand what else matters to them.

Understanding who and what influences your ideal buyer

You need a clear understanding of your buyer, not just which retailers you plan to target, but the person or people – the actual individuals who are responsible for selecting and buying products or services such as yours. This is not the same as the pen-portrait of 'Alan' that I shared earlier; this isn't about who is your ideal customer, this is now about a real buyer in a real retail business.

When I talk about clearly understanding the buyer I mean having insight into how buying your product or service can make their job easier; what's in it for them both in terms of meeting their own work objectives and on a more personal level too.

In the first instance you do need to identify the retailers you intend to approach – so by knowing your ideal customer/end user, you will be able to determine which retailers are most likely to want to buy from you. You should create a list and prioritize them so that you have a clear action plan for the next part of the book, Pitch Big.

Next, you need to do some research to understand which departments, teams and roles have an influence on, input to, or responsibility for the decision to select and purchase products or services such as yours. This is quite challenging and may involve online research, reading company reports and news releases, even trawling through social networks (again, LinkedIn would probably be best for this) to understand who does what. It's important that you learn as much as you can about your potential retail customer, as retailers often have quite different organizational structures. You will need to review each retailer that you plan to approach in order to ensure that you've got clarity about who the parties are that will be instrumental in the decision to buy from you.

It will also be useful to understand a bit more about their reward structure; for instance, if buyers are offered bonuses for achieving targets, what are the targets that they are working towards? As you discover snippets of information you can begin to build a picture of 'what's in it for them' in terms of your buyer's business targets as well as how that impacts them personally and financially. This means that when it comes to the preparation stage of 'Pitch Big', you'll be able to formulate a compelling proposition for a buyer based on how your product or service enables them to achieve their targets. It's also wise to understand the retailer's current position – what products or services do they currently have which your offer could be a replacement for or an enhancement to? Knowing what already exists within the retail business will demonstrate a thorough understanding of your potential customer, putting you in a stronger and better-informed position when you are planning your pitch.

We'll explore this concept further in Chapter 7 on preparation. For now, the key message I want to leave with you is that you can never know too much about your potential customer and the business environment they are working in. If you spend some time thinking about this now, and considering what you already know, what you will need to know, and where you can get that information from, then, when it comes to the next part on Pitch Big, you will have many of the elements you need to support the pre-sales preparation.

Now, and before we move off the topic of customer and on to the topic of competition, we need to explore your pricing in a little more detail. While pricing is part of your positioning relative to your competitive set, it is in fact your customer who needs to be influenced by, and respond to, your pricing. That's why I've included it in this chapter and not in the next.

Pricing – a key part of your positioning

You must remember that whatever you are selling, price is a part of your positioning and you need to get it right. If you sell a quality product, have a higher-end brand proposition and also deliver excellent service, the buyer will expect you to be a bit more expensive; if you're not they'll wonder why, they'll question your long-term viability – they've been around long enough to understand that suppliers also need to make money to survive. Retailers have, in the past, been accused of being too aggressive on price, but in recent years most of them have realized that long-term partnerships with good suppliers give them a more consistent, stable supply-base. They understand that suppliers need to make a fair profit to remain able to supply them, so underpricing will be as likely to raise concerns in the mind of a buyer as being too expensive.

That said, they will still only select products that present a solid commercial proposition. You need to price your product or service such that it provides the retailer with good margins or a tangible return on investment.

Service providers need to really think through their pricing to ensure that their business model is viable, sufficiently competitive to meet scrutiny versus other providers *and* is not based on what it costs you to supply the service but is based on the value you bring. This approach to pricing of services, based on cost not value, is a trap that many smaller businesses fall into. It's one to be avoided. When you are a small business and your overheads are low you might think you can get away with pricing low, to win business on price. In the long run that's not ideal as someone will always be willing to undercut you, and when you've won customers who are only interested in price they won't stay loyal, they'll go with the cheapest provider. In addition, as your business grows, becomes more complex, you'll need to be generating more margin per sale in order to pay for the higher costs of running a bigger business.

With product pricing you need to bear in mind the ideal retail price, your cost price, your margin, and make sure that in the 'chain' there is adequate capacity to offer the retailer a cost price which enables them to meet their targets too. If you are selling products, don't underestimate the margin that retailers want to achieve. This point was echoed by both Emma Wimhurst and Neil Westwood, with Emma saying:

> To add your product to their range a retailer has to make space in stores by taking something else off. You need to prove that your product can deliver more margin than other items. The retailers' margin expectations were a major issue in the early days at Diva. Most consumers/business owners have no idea that retailers are targeting 50–60 per cent margin, minimum, as well as asking for listing fees (a one-off charge some retailers ask suppliers to pay before they will introduce their item to their range). It's all about the retailer being able to maximize margin per square foot of selling space. As a supplier, knowing the details of your finances is critical – your cost price, your walk-away points etc.

and with Neil simply saying:

> I didn't know that the retailers would want to achieve at least two-times mark-up – this came as a bit of a shock!

So when it comes to pricing, what you need to remember is that the better the deal you can give, the more likely it will be that the retailer will consider your items. Certainly it balances the risk in the mind of the retail buyer – they'll be more likely to take a risk on a new product because the margin opportunity is excellent compared to other items.

If the difference is too little they're unlike to consider eliminating existing, proven items to make way for yours. Chances are that the buyer is targeted on achieving a certain level of margin or return on space for their retail business. If they make their targets they get a bonus, a good performance review, maybe even a promotion; if they don't they are putting their own career prospects and earning potential at risk. So it's not really about the buyer being ruthless on price, it's about what's in it for them. If you put yourself in their shoes you'd probably be doing the same.

Product pricing – calculations

When it comes to product pricing I have a simple calculator that I use with clients; it's based in Excel. I've outlined it in Figure 4.2 and explained each of the steps and calculations. This is also available for download from the resources area via **www.retailchampion.co.uk/selling-to-retailers/resources** as an Excel spreadsheet, complete with the formulae.

FIGURE 4.2 Product margin, mark-up and RRP calculator

RRP	RRP ex VAT	Retailer cost price	Retailer cash margin	Retailer % margin	Retail mark-up	Your cost price	Your cash margin	Your % margin	TOTAL CHAIN MARGIN %
£599	£499.17	£250	£249.17	50%	2×	£145	£105	42%	71%

Terminology:

- RRP: recommended retail price – the ideal price that your product should be sold for; this includes VAT where the item incurs VAT (you need to check the prevailing rate for VAT for your specific product).

- RRP ex VAT: the retail price net of VAT; this is the true revenue the retailer receives when it makes a sale of the item, as the VAT is of course owed to HMRC (in the UK).

- Retailer cost price: this is the cost price that the retailer pays you for the item, otherwise known as your selling price.

- Retailer cash margin: this is the difference between the RRP ex VAT and the retailer cost price – the proportion of the total sales revenue which is essentially 'earned' by the retailer when it sells an item. This value is important to a retailer as it is the sum of cash margin that goes to pay for all of its business overheads, staff, premises, costs etc and what's left is profit.

- Retailer % margin: this is the cash margin expressed as a percentage of the RRP ex VAT – a measure used to assess the importance of a product, as the higher the % margin a product can produce the more likely retailers will be to include it in their ranges.

- Retail mark-up: another way of expressing the importance of a product; the mark-up is the multiplication factor that would be applied to the retailer cost price to achieve the RRP ex VAT – the higher the number, the more value each sale contributes to the retailer's business.

- Your cost price: this is what it costs you to produce the product, and should include the shipping costs. Usually an average allowance for shipping is added to the product actual cost. This may vary with different order quantities and so you may need to create different margin calculator scenarios for different retail minimum order quantities.

- Your cash margin: similar to the retail margin, this is the difference between the retailer cost price (your selling price) and your cost price.

- Your % margin: this is your cash margin expressed as a % of your selling price.

- Total chain margin %: this is the total cash margin in the 'chain' (your margin plus the retailer margin) expressed as a % of the RRP. It shows how hard the product has to 'work' to deliver benefit to both your business and your retail customer.

Linked to pricing is a focus on your product costings – obviously these impact your cost price. You need to know your product costings inside out, understanding each of the factors that influence the cost price, and have detailed monitoring in place. When you upscale, if you don't have tight control on costs you could discover that you're not achieving the margins you expected or need. It will also help you in Chapter 9 on negotiation, because when a retailer has expressed interest in your product and wants to enter into a cost price negotiation with you, you need to really understand the impact of, for instance, offering a higher minimum order quantity to meet the retailer's target unit price. Therefore, while the margin calculator I've shared is a simple tool, if your costs can reduce as your order quantity increases then you can add scenarios into your margin calculator to help you derive the unit cost price for the retailer based on different order quantity commitments. Having this sort of information at your fingertips will really support you when it comes to negotiations.

Before we move on, I suggest that you spend a little time preparing your margin calculator so that you've at least got a first attempt at it; you can develop this further over time. If you already know what the price-breaks are for volume orders you can add these in as scenarios; if not, make a note to investigate this and see if it has any economies of scale that would enable it to offer you a better price for a larger order quantity.

Wrapping up

In this chapter we have considered your customer – the end user, who the product or service is for, and the buyer, the person who transacts the purchase with you. We have explored how to:

- identify better with your end user and really have a detailed understanding of who they are;
- understand the key concerns of your buyer, ensuring that when it comes to pitching big you will be better prepared to demonstrate why, with your proposition, they have nothing to worry about;
- price your product or service so that it's a viable, value-adding proposition, both for your buyer and for your business.

In the next chapter we'll look at your competition. Knowing the ins and outs of their business proposition, product offer, pricing and positioning will arm you with everything you need to consider when you come on to the next part of the book, Pitch Big.

Competition

05

Introduction

In this chapter we're going to be taking a detailed look at your competition. This is linked to, and a development of, the analysis you did when determining how you were positioned relative to the competitive set.

First, we'll look at competitor analysis using a technique called Porter's Five Forces, which is extremely beneficial for you to understand your marketplace better. It will help you decide if you should be developing an offer in a specific market, or if it is too heavily contested.

Then we'll discuss why you need to know your competition at all. We'll consider what you really need to know about them and how you can leverage that insight to your advantage, ensuring you have a comprehensive knowledge of your competition in terms of:

- Why they are competition: what is it that they offer that could be considered to be an alternative choice to what you offer?
- What they offer: what are their quality standards and their service levels? What is their pricing and their value proposition?
- Who they sell to: who are their customers? Can you get hold of case studies? Do they appear to have a niche?
- Where they sell: what routes to market do they sell through? Are they only selling locally or do they sell internationally?
- How do they sell: what techniques do they use? Do they access conferences and events? Trade shows? E-mail marketing? E-commerce? Tele-marketing? Etc.
- Are there any 'cracks' in their proposition? Can you identify any specifics where you can confidently demonstrate that your offer excels/surpasses that of the competition?

All of this analysis and understanding will benefit you in the next part of the book: Pitch Big.

Competitor analysis

When it comes to competitor analysis you should ideally be under-taking a review of the market on a regular basis – quarterly or half-yearly at least. The market evolves, competitors come and go, and it's important you stay abreast of the market, aware of the competition, both right now and in terms of what may be coming up in the future.

The first step is to complete some research about the market as a whole. If you have not yet started up, it's critical you know the market you plan to enter. If you are already trading you need to understand the dynamics. If you plan to launch a new brand, new products or services, or enter new territories (international markets, for example), you really need to do the research to avoid it being a disaster.

You will also be expected to include evidence of rigorous competi-tor analysis as part of your business plan if you ever attempt to raise finance from a bank or from an investor. They'll need to have confi-dence that you have done the research, understood the market, how heavily contested it is, and therefore have a robust basis for the claims you will be making about your forecast turnover. Of course, the reason is that they'll need to trust that your claims about what return on investment or payback period they can expect are substantiated in detailed, realistic analysis.

I'd never condone launching a business – service based or product-centric – without having a comprehensive understanding of that market: it would be madness! You could be wasting your time and money and your business could fail. Alternatively, if the market is wide open and you've spotted a gap, you need to be ready to go for it in a *big* way! If you don't go for it deeply enough, corner the market and secure the maximum market share at the outset, your brilliant idea could be overrun with new entrants following suit. Your opportunity to lead the market, achieve high growth and benefit from the associated financial reward would be lost.

So a strategic view is important, as is an ongoing review, because one thing you can guarantee is that it will change. As your business grows, becomes better known, more established, you will find that those you considered competition in the past may not be as relevant to you anymore and other brands will come into the frame. You need to be mindful that ongoing competitor analysis – knowing the market and the threat of competition – also forms a critical part of the final section of the 12-point plan too: get big and stay big!

I'm going to introduce you to an approach known as Porter's Five Forces, which is a fairly well known and simple technique that is as relevant to a new start-up as it is to a global mega-brand. There are far more complex models that you can use, but this should be adequate for most businesses. I want to give you a flavour of this method before we then drill into the detail of your specific competitors, how you can get a better understanding of them, and why you need that knowledge when it comes to the next part of the book, Pitch Big.

Porter's Five Forces analysis

I first came across this technique many years ago when studying the marketing component of a professional diploma in purchasing and supply chain management. I've found it to be a simple tool, relevant to my own small business as well as applicable to my clients' businesses. As a tool it's great because it really doesn't matter what you do or how big you are, it is still applicable. If you are interested in this approach you can find lots of background about it online. By way of introduction, Porter's Five Forces analysis is a method of understanding the market in which you trade; essentially it helps you work out the overview of your competitive landscape. It was created in 1979 by Michael E Porter of Harvard Business School and has been referenced ever since.

In his approach Porter stated that there are five influencing factors, the forces, which affect a market. These are:

1 The threat of new entrants to the market becoming new competition.

2 The threat of your customers moving away from your offer, buying into substitute products or services.

3 The strength of the customer's position in a negotiation, the 'bargaining power' of the buyer.

4 The strength of the supplier's position in a negotiation, the 'bargaining power' of the seller.

5 These four factors all then contribute to the fifth – the intensity of competitive rivalry, how saturated the market is for the product or service, how contested the market is in terms of the fight to win customers.

This is often portrayed as a diagram (Figure 5.1) that shows how the forces act together to define the competitive landscape within which your business trades. The threat of new entrants and substitution 'squeeze' the market, making it tougher for you to trade as there is a great deal of choice for the customer. The power balance of buyer and supplier is all about supply and demand, push–pull, creating a tug-of-war between each end of the supply chain. In the middle is your market, or what's left of it after being pushed, pulled and squeezed! It's within this market that you have to have confidence that you can operate successfully. This is a powerful way of deciding if you really do have an opportunity or if you should maybe explore markets where the forces are less aggressive, thus making the intensity of competitive rivalry much gentler; a far better set of conditions in which a business can thrive, I am sure you'd agree.

FIGURE 5.1 Porter's Five Forces

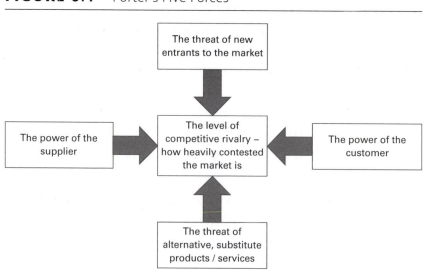

Using Porter's Five Forces you can analyse if an opportunity really exists for you in the current market. If you do this kind of market analysis, there are detailed considerations for each of the five elements to bear in mind. Let's look at those now and consider what each means. It's not an exhaustive list, and you can probably think of more. In the main, these are common sense:

1 **Threat of new entrants**: When a market is either profitable or new, it is obviously going to make that market more attractive to new entrants. Chances are that if you are considering entering a market because it's 'hot', you will not be alone. Of course, the impact is that the opportunity quickly becomes eroded as more new entrants take up market share, diluting the market for all. If something looks like it's the next big thing, unless you've got the financial backing to enter the market aggressively, securing as much share as you can and as quickly as possible, it may not be worth the risk. There will be far bigger companies, with much deeper pockets, eager to corner the market and cut out smaller competition. Other considerations include:

   a Any barriers to entry that might exist; patents are one example – if an organization owns the rights to a particular capability (be that a product or a service), it is very difficult to get around that. This is something we have seen in recent years as technology companies try to get into the smartphone market where Apple has been dominant. Many have found that as Apple has secured international patents on a wide range of capabilities, other brands are prevented from developing anything similar.

   b If this market benefits from economies of scale, established brands in a market will already have volumes that enable them to trade considerably more profitably than a smaller entrant could. In this case it may be too risky for a new entrant to come into that market, as the pricing it will need to achieve to match the competition and to be a viable proposition in the customers' view may render it non-profitable. This can be seen in the lower end of the clothing sector – supermarkets have been able to retail clothing at such low price points that there is no place for smaller clothing retailers at the lower, economy end of the market. This means that the market polarizes, with big brands leveraging economies of scale, dominating the economy market, and with smaller brands having to position at the higher end, where price is not the decision factor in the eyes of the customer and thus where economy of scale isn't a barrier.

c Brand equity can be a barrier if customers are predominantly loyal to established brands in a market.

d Start-up costs and ongoing costs can prevent new entrants, especially where there is a significant overhead to enter a new market. This is further emphasized owing to sources of funding for new businesses having become much more limited since the global financial crisis.

e Access to distribution can be a barrier, in particular if the majority of new entrants would have difficulty in reaching the customer, owing to logistics barriers.

f A final, more positive consideration, is any government incentive to attract more entrants to a market. If there is a policy to encourage entrants to a new sector, including grants and other support, there will be an increased number of entrants – great if you are one of them, not if you are already established in a market!

2 **Threat of alternatives/substitutes:** As the saying goes, 'there is more than one way to skin a cat' and that's why alternatives and substitutes are a threat in a market. If you are thirsty and want a cold drink you have umpteen brands available to you – each a substitute for the next. This is subtly different from choosing between very similar products – eg two different brands of orange juice – that's a direct competitor. A substitute could be lemonade or mineral water – it solves the customer's desire to quench their thirst but is not part of the orange juice market. We will consider competitors offering products that could be selected as a viable alternative to yours later in the chapter when we dig into the more detailed understanding of your competition. Other considerations for this area of Porter's Five Forces are:

a How likely will a buyer be to consider a substitute? Is the market one with a wide choice of solutions to the buyer's need or is it a very specific need? Are there a high or low number of substitute products available in the market?

b Does choosing a substitute offer the buyer a better price, an item with better quality attributes, or better performance? Does the buyer have sufficient understanding of, and recognize the differences between, the product offered and the alternative item?

c Are there any benefits as a result of substitution that would mean that, for instance, the total cost of ownership is preferential to the buyer?

3 Power of the customer: When the customer has great influence over the seller this can often be referred to as a 'buyers' market'. Depending on various factors, your market is influenced by the relative power your customers have to influence your pricing and your sales potential:

a The most obvious one to consider is supply versus demand (number of buyers versus availability of supply). The greater the supply and the lower the demand, the more choice customers have, so they are in a stronger position to negotiate with a supplier, knowing that the supplier needs their custom.

b Is the customer able to access alternative sources? Where a customer only has access to a restricted number of sources of supply then clearly suppliers offering that access are in a stronger position than those which the customer cannot reach.

c Another key factor is the size of buyer (also known as buying power) versus the size of seller and how important the buyer is to the seller. When a buyer is a larger entity and a seller is a smaller entity, often the buyer can leverage this in negotiation to press the supplier to accept terms more favourable to the buyer. The buyer will consider that their custom is of more significant importance to the seller. This can only be reversed when a small seller has a product that the buyer really wants and there is no other source of supply (as we'll see in the final point in this list).

d When buyers have greater access to product information, which is something that the internet has enabled, they are more able to compare similar products in great detail. With access to information, the buyer has the power to choose where to buy based on a much greater array of content. Buyers no longer have to depend on the seller's brochure/marketing materials but can reference content from other customers, reviews and product specification details to support their decision making.

e When a buyer is particularly price sensitive, they will choose to buy from the lowest-cost supplier. This is transactional behaviour versus loyal behaviour. Transactional customers always seek out the best price and this is a primary decision factor. Loyal customers are engaged by the whole brand proposition and will buy from the brand they identify with most, irrespective of price.

f Finally, as touched on above, when the supplier has a highly desirable product which the buyer wants, and when there are limited sources for a buyer to obtain a product, the buyer's power to negotiate or influence the purchase is much reduced.

4 Power of the supplier: In the same way that a customer can have the balance of power in a decision or transaction, so can the supplier. Many considerations we made regarding the power of the customer apply to the supplier; it's a case of looking at the same point from the alternative perspective:

a As above, supply versus demand considerations – when there is limited supply and greater demand the supplier can wield greater power.

b As above, sources of supply – when you sell what customers want and there are limited sources, then as the supplier you have the stronger position.

c As above, size of buyer versus size of seller, from the perspective of a smaller buyer and larger supplier.

d And a consideration not accounted for above is the ability of the supplier to cut out its customer and go direct to consumers (very relevant to the product sector, less applicable for services). This is something retailers in particular are mindful of when buying from brands. Obviously, and as we covered in the previous chapter when we looked at pricing, there is a far greater margin opportunity for a supplier who can cut out the need for retailers as distribution channels and sell direct to the end user. That said, without considerable investment in channels and marketing, the majority of brands would never manage to achieve the market penetration and reach on their own that they can achieve by working with retailers.

5 **Competitive rivalry**: All of the prior four factors determine the level of competitive rivalry within an industry or a market. This element is really about understanding the state of the market, when all of the other four factors are working together, to define the market overall and to assess if it is an attractive proposition.

As I said before, this is a good technique to use *before* you start a business, launch a new brand, develop a new product or service, or enter a new territory.

Now it's time to get a much more detailed view of your competition.

Why you need to know your competition

In the introduction to this chapter I listed a whole host of things you need to know about your competition. We're now going to take a moment to consider *why* it's worth knowing them and how that will benefit you in the process of planning your approach to retail buyers.

The idea behind all of this is quite simple. If you know as much as you possibly can about your competition then, should you be quizzed by a retailer about why they should buy from you as opposed to someone else, this insight into your competition will give you the confidence to state the reasons why. You will know that your answers are based on facts and you can highlight your points of differentiation.

In such circumstances, knowing the competition means you can focus the buyer onto your unique position, the advantages of your offering, your specific points of differentiation and your value proposition. Without being explicit about your competition's failings you will be able to highlight the particular points of differentiation between your brand and theirs.

Leveraging your points of difference is applicable both in terms of the marketing materials you produce and any conversations you may have with a buyer. When you know which attributes of your product/service or proposition can excel over the competition, you can highlight these to a buyer.

It's this awareness of where your brand stands out, your differentiators, and your confidence in your position that will really aid you in the selling process. Wherever the buyer happens across your information – in print, online or in conversation – you will have given them food for thought, sown a seed of doubt, which perhaps makes them feel the need to investigate further. A buyer would not be doing a good job if they didn't compare your proposition to the competition – it's a requirement of their role to do this, just like you would if you were considering using a tradesperson in your home or if you were buying a new mobile phone handset. Now you've put them in mind of an attribute where you excel, if that is something important to them then they are going to investigate further and discover that you are the best choice in the market. You, of course, already knew that thanks to your detailed knowledge of your competition.

Finally, another reason why this kind of market knowledge is beneficial is if a buyer seems to be giving you the brush-off, in particular if they believe that they have what you offer from another source, an incumbent supplier. Don't forget, changing supplier is not only extra work for the buyer in terms of the administration involved, it's also going to affect the working relationships that they will have developed over time with their existing supplier. Buyers may initially give you the brush-off because it's too much trouble – they're reasonably happy with what they have got and believe it's the same as what you offer. Why would they create extra work for themselves? Knowing about your competition (and in this scenario focusing specifically on their incumbent supplier), you can again leverage your points of differentiation, your unique selling points (USP), in order to try to get the buyer to pay a bit more attention to you. By highlighting your strengths, and thus by subtly raising doubts with the buyer about their existing supplier, you may well get a chance to present to them.

A word of caution, however, before we move on to the next section. In my opinion, you should *never* say or print anything that is directly and explicitly drawing a comparison between you and a competitor. At best it seems like a 'cheap shot' – you can't find enough good to say about yourself so you have to revert to saying something demeaning about someone else. You don't want to be seen as that sort of person in business. At worst it can get you into a serious legal battle with a disgruntled competitor who may say you are making false claims or damaging their brand/reputation. While you may absolutely *know* that you could make a claim, and you believe it could make the difference to the sale, my perspective is that if you can maintain integrity and focus on your strengths you will form better business relationships and develop a better reputation, which is more valuable for the long term. While it may be infuriating, and you may be eager to explain why a competitor is perhaps overselling themselves, you should try to keep it to yourself. Julie Meyer, a self-made multi-millionaire entrepreneur who runs Ariadne Capital, an investment company, says in her talks, 'Don't treat losers like losers' – keep that in mind and maintain the more superior position.

Understanding the competition

When it comes to understanding the competition and knowing the ins and outs of their business model, offer, pricing and positioning will arm you with everything you need to be mindful of when you come on to the next part of the book, Pitch Big.

In the introduction to this chapter I listed six things you need to understand about your competition. Now it's time to think about *how* you can get this information and what you might do with it. Figure 5.2 explores each of the six areas outlined in the introduction in more detail.

FIGURE 5.2 Understanding the competition

What you need to know	How to get this information	What you can use it for
Why they are competition – what is it that they offer that could be considered to be an alternative choice to what you offer?	You need to identify all possible suppliers of products or services that can provide the same end-use as yours, or which would be an effective alternative. Then analyse their offer compared to yours. Make sure you think like your ideal customer – would they give the product/service serious consideration as an alternative to what you offer? If so, you need to add the company offering the product/service to your list of confirmed competitors. If in doubt keep them on the list – better to be aware of them at this stage and rule them out later than to miss something important!	At this stage, knowing that there is a potential alternative to you on the market 'opens your eyes' and it means that you can continue with the rest of the analysis mindful of the whole picture. The biggest failing you could make at this stage is overlooking or disregarding a potential competitor, as your analysis would be incomplete. As is the nature of such things, the inevitable would happen – the one you'd overlooked would be exactly the one you needed to be most aware of.
What they offer – what are their quality standards and their service levels? What is their pricing and their value proposition?	Most of this information should be available in their brochures or on their website. You can always call and pretend to be interested, asking that they send you further details. If that doesn't work, see if they plan to be exhibiting at any trade shows – these are often free to visit and you may discover many of your competitors under one roof. You can browse their stands, collect their marketing materials and talk to their staff at these shows (but don't forget, they can do all of these things to you too!).	When you have a detailed side-by-side comparison of your proposition versus the competition, you can begin to identify areas where they excel and where you excel. This benefits you in two ways: 1) you could potentially improve areas of your proposition where the competition is stronger; 2) you can leverage this insight to define your specific points of difference, which is very useful, as touched on already, when presenting your offer to a retailer in a situation where there are other suppliers (your competition) in the frame.

FIGURE 5.2 *continued*

What you need to know	How to get this information	What you can use it for
Who they sell to – who are their customers? Can you get hold of case studies? Do they appear to have a niche?	In many cases a list of their customers would be on their website – for service providers it's often on a 'client case studies' page, for product suppliers it's often 'our distributors'. They may explicitly state that they have a niche, or that may be apparent from the customer base. If customers aren't listed online it will be more difficult to find this out, but again, a cheeky call to them to ask 'and what sort of businesses buy your product/service?', might just get an answer. Otherwise an online search may reveal some press releases (from them or from their customers) stating that they're working together.	If you know who already have products or services from your competition, you can focus on those who don't – it's a lot easier to get your foot in the door with a retailer who doesn't already have a supplier offering a similar proposition to yours. It may transpire that your ideal customer is a customer of your competition, in which case review your key points of difference – having that knowledge and ability to prepare will be fundamental to success.
Where they sell – what routes to market do they sell through? Are they only selling locally or do they sell internationally?	Again, much of this information is likely to be on their website or in their brochure.	Knowing where your competition sell will help you identify if there are untapped markets or channels which you could leverage. International is a very interesting consideration, certainly one I always explore with my clients. In recent years the UK has been particularly keen to support British businesses with overseas expansion. Many other governments are supporting businesses to increase their overall export business too.

FIGURE 5.2 *continued*

What you need to know	How to get this information	What you can use it for
How do they sell – what techniques do they use? Conferences and events? Trade shows? E-mail marketing? E-commerce? Tele-marketing? etc.	A search online for their company, brand or product/ service name should reveal a number of the methods they use. You won't necessarily be able to identify everything, not initially, but if you get the option to enquire online, for instance, you can learn a lot about their follow-up methods and how they use e-mail or tele-marketing.	Knowing how they sell, and how successful they are, can help you define your approach to selling. You can learn from the best parts of what your competition do and from the example set by an array of your most successful competition. It will also potentially highlight techniques less well used by the competition, which might be an opportunity for you to leverage a lesser-used technique to reach buyers in a way that is less 'saturated'.
Are there any 'cracks' in their proposition? Can you identify any specifics where you can confidently demonstrate that your offer excels/surpasses that of the competition?	This final element of the analysis is really a review of everything that you've gleaned from all the elements you've covered. Determining how you fare in a side-by-side comparison to your key competitors will help you to distil the key aspects that you should focus on and equally those that you are best to avoid.	This summary of insight can be leveraged in all your sales and marketing activities. You can blow your trumpet about your points of difference, and sow seeds of doubt about your competition in the areas where you know you excel.

So now the onus is on you to go and discover everything you might ever need to know about your competition!

Wrapping up

In this chapter we have looked in detail at your competition. We have:

- reviewed a very useful method of market competitiveness analysis using Porter's Five Forces model;
- considered why it's really important to know and understand your direct competition in detail;
- analysed your competition to ensure that you know who they are and, more importantly, how you can differentiate from them, which will be hugely beneficial when you move to Part Three: Pitch Big.

In the next chapter we'll look at your scalability. This falls into the part on Plan Big because if you don't plan to upscale to big retailer demands you'll almost certainly fail your customers at some point in the future. With that in mind, let's move on to this final chapter in the part on Plan Big.

06 Scalability

Introduction

In this chapter we'll be considering how you can plan to upscale your business operations to ensure that when you deliver your winning pitch (in the next part of the book) you're ready to deliver on your promises too!

Scalability is all about ensuring you have all the necessary ingredients in place and ready to 'switch on', to ensure that when a major retailer agrees a deal with you *nothing* will be a barrier to your ability to fulfil their requirement and secure a new, happy customer.

In this chapter we're going to look at what underpins your business scalability, focusing on:

- What scalability is all about: ensuring you start with the end in mind, developing a robust business model with repeatable processes, managing risks and being able to grow securely.

- The importance of planning your supply chain and making sure you've got the capability to deliver on your promises. In this part we'll also look at managing risk/compliance and consider things such as your ethical and environmental policies – all the issues *big* companies are fearful of getting caught out on and that could cause them to pull out of an order if you or your supply chain were found to be non-compliant.

- Managing cash flow in the early days: often retailers' buying terms will mean that payment can be around 90 days after receipt of the order – you need to make sure you've got that kind of cash flow impact covered, securing funding if necessary.

- Protection of your business, your brand and your ideas, as in order to really scale your business you need to prevent and avoid copycats.

Scalability touches on your business processes, supplier relationships, logistics, finances and brand protection. However, you could summarize it in just one phrase – risk management – and this chapter is all about how you prepare your business to be ready to manage the risks inherent to any growing business.

What is scalability all about?

I said earlier 'start with the end in mind' and that's something key to consider in all that you do. Before we dig into detail I want to spend a moment to explain why, at this planning stage, you already need to be thinking about growth in such detail. The fact is that no retail business will buy from you unless you can demonstrate how you are able to scale up to support their demands reliably. If you are selling products, then once the retailer has introduced your product to their customers they will have set an expectation with their customers that they will have your product available and to a consistent quality standard. They expect you, as the supplier, to enable them to meet that promise to their customer. If you are selling services, they will expect your business to have the ability to cope with their needs and be aligned to their business operations. This may include things like a 24/7 helpline or nationwide (possibly even international) on-site service coverage.

As you can imagine, having all these plans in place upfront, before you present to a retailer, means that you'll have answers to the questions that they are likely to ask. Moreover, being readily able to answer difficult questions about capacities and contingency plans will give the retailer far greater confidence in you, your business and your professionalism. You will make a better overall impression on the retailer and you will feel like a 'safer bet' than perhaps another small business which simply hasn't done an adequate level of planning.

Robust and repeatable processes and systems

The key ingredient to becoming scalable is developing your business, from the outset, with growth in mind. This also enables you to become a replicable business, which we explore in more detail in Chapter 11 on replication. In my own mission statement I talk about helping business owners to develop robust and repeatable processes and systems to enable them to become scalable, saleable businesses. What I mean by this is:

- Robust: simple, clear processes that any member of staff, regardless of experience, can follow. Removing ambiguity, removing risk of failure, ensuring that even when the business is under pressure the key activities continue to perform. A robust business doesn't crumble when there is a stressful situation. It responds and copes.

- Repeatable: your robust processes enable your whole organization to continually deliver on your promises, to a consistent quality standard, time and again.

- Processes and systems: this encompasses all of the day-to-day actions, interactions, transactions and analysis your business needs to be doing to operate and deliver on your customer promise. These are done by either your people or your suppliers, or are automated – done by computer processors.

- Scalable: this is very important – the crux of this chapter. This is about utilizing the robust and repeatable processes that you've created so that you can grow your business without *you* becoming a bottleneck! When you're a scalable business you're able to walk away, having delegated to others, with the confidence that the business will operate effectively, and to your standards, without you. A scalable business is one that a retail buyer will have confidence to buy from; they will appreciate that it is a well-oiled machine, with all the necessary ingredients in place to ramp up, if necessary, and be able to support that retailer in achieving its aims.

- Saleable: a saleable business is one that has a value in the eyes of a dispassionate, outside observer. That could be investors, a bank or a business/individual seeking to acquire other businesses. It doesn't mean that the business is for sale; it means that the business owner has successfully created a business that encompasses robust and repeatable processes and is therefore scalable and can operate without that business owner at the helm.

If you can prove that your business is scalable, you'll be reassuring any retail buyer that they can have confidence in doing business with you. Without securing their confidence it won't matter how good your proposition is, they will be reluctant to buy from you as they will always have the concern that you may fail to deliver on your promises, which in turn will cause them to fail on theirs. No retail buyer is going to risk their job, their income and their security by selecting a supplier that seems a bit fragile or unprepared, so please bear this in mind and ensure that you give this chapter the focus it deserves.

You need to spend some time to ensure that your business processes are robust and repeatable. Test them out – see what you think and be honest with yourself. I am sure you will find areas that need improvement and other aspects where you've got it right. As you develop ways of working you may initially start out with a manual process that is more time consuming and requires skill – that's fine, so long as you plan how, once you've refined and embedded a process, you can make it more efficient. Knowing that in order to be scalable you need all of your processes to be robust and repeatable, I'd suggest that a key part of your growth plans should be centred on reviewing your current business operating model and identifying how you can improve it. As you develop new processes you should be mindful that while what you do now may be manual, you do intend to make it either more automated, or simpler, or more efficient in future.

The next consideration for a scalable business is not just what you do internally but how your whole supply chain performs to deliver your proposition, so we'll now take a look at the supply chain.

Planning the supply chain

Depending on your offering you will likely have some form of supply chain. Even if you have a service proposition your supply chain will still involve all the 'actors in the process' that enable you to deliver that service. They may not be making things or shipping boxes but, for instance, if you develop technology or software your equivalent of the manufacturing element of a product supply chain would be the team of developers, programmers, testers and other skilled people who can translate the requirements into a usable tool. Each of those parties adds their input to the process in a sequence, just like a product on a manufacturing line. The output has to be to the quality standard you've promised and delivered to the customer, one way or another, on time. Therefore, the principles of supply chain planning that we'll consider here are applicable to both product and services suppliers. What we're going to look at in this section is more about understanding capacities, lead time, logistics, managing information flow, removing risk from the process, and knowing where the limitations lie.

Breaking down each of the elements listed above – capacities, lead time, logistics and information flow – Figure 6.1 highlights what you need to know about each and why, in order to have a clearer picture of your current scalability and what you might be able to do to increase that, if required, in future.

FIGURE 6.1 Supply chain scalability – key considerations

Consideration	What you need to know	Future actions to improve
Capacity: this is your ability to create output within a timeframe based on your current infrastructure.	It's imperative that you know what you can and cannot ask of your supply chain – so you need to know what the maximum output is by hour, day, week etc. You also need to understand when there is planned downtime (Chinese New Year is usually one to watch for those who manufacture in the Far East). Knowing this enables you to confirm what you can or cannot deliver, and in what timeframe, to a retail buyer.	When you understand the current constraints and limitations on your capacity, you can review options to increase that by adding in additional resources, shifts, manufacturing lines or whatever you need. It's also worth reviewing local versus offshore options and third-party providers who might be able to give you a temporary boost in capacity, to overcome peaks in demand, that could be secured on a short-term, non-permanent basis.

FIGURE 6.1 *continued*

Consideration	What you need to know	Future actions to improve
Lead time: this is the sum of the timeline of activities that have to be completed from receipt of an order/ contract to successful delivery of the product or services.	You need to understand each and every step of the process and how long it takes in order to understand not only the entire lead time but also which aspects might be accelerated if there was a need to do so. You should be breaking the process down into a detailed step-by-step flow in order to understand the bottlenecks, risks and opportunities to increase efficiency.	Only when you really understand the lead time can you look to improve it. For instance, you may learn that from the point of order it takes five days for the manufacturer to acknowledge the order – if you can get them to acknowledge it on the same day you can cut five days out of your lead time. Other ideas that help accelerate lead time could be holding stock of raw materials so production can begin immediately rather than waiting for raw materials to be delivered. It all really depends on what your unique process is.
Logistics: this is the physical movement of goods, or the implementation of services, that has to be undertaken to complete your service promise.	Depending on your commercial arrangements, you or third parties in your supply chain may be responsible for the actual logistics of delivering your product or services. You need to know who is responsible for each step and ensure that it is being done to the timeline which underpins your lead time. You also need a mechanism by which any issues can be reported to you so you can take action to resolve them. If you don't know the lead time you certainly can't commit to a delivery date, so this information is critical.	The ability of the logistics flow to adhere to the process timeline is often the reason for late delivery or increased costs. You can reduce the impact and improve the process by taking advantage of collaboration tools that help remote parties involved in projects and processes keep each other informed on progress. Such a capability will become important to you as your business grows, so it makes sense to begin to embed this as early on as possible in order that it is an established set of behaviours – before it becomes an issue.

FIGURE 6.1   *continued*

Consideration	What you need to know	Future actions to improve
Information flow: this is the sharing of updates, statuses and relevant communications with *all* parties involved in the whole process – from the customer to all those in the supply chain.	Linked to the lead time and the logistics, the information flow really is all about who needs to know what and when. What information is needed to support timely decisions that enable the supply chain to operate effectively and meet the promises you made to your retail customer? Don't forget, your customer, the retail buyer, may also want to receive updates from you – and when they do you need to be armed with all of the facts.	Also linked to the above, collaboration and project management tools do help the information flow. You may also consider webinar and remote meeting technologies if you have parties spread out around the world. It's imperative that if there is ever a failure in your supply chain, you have a debrief, invite everyone to comment, and from that identify what needs to change to avoid issues in the future. Only by having an open and frank communications and information flow can you expect optimal ongoing performance.

Of course, managing the supply chain isn't only about the risks; it's about being able to meet the retailers' stringent requirements for service delivery. You're more than likely to be asked to sign a service level agreement. For product suppliers this can include specifics around pallet loading, packaging sizes, label positions and meeting your allocated time slot for delivery. There may well be penalties for failing to achieve complete and on-time delivery and you may find that if your delivery isn't perfectly presented it will be turned away. Many retailers operate fully automated warehousing, so products must be delivered and labelled to comply with their instructions or the system can't handle the items.

For service suppliers, similar requirements around your service delivery may be imposed; you may well be expected to provide (if you don't already) 24/7 helplines, access to support staff, maybe even on-site support with a rapid response time. Modern retailers are dealing with customers 24/7 and can't afford any kind of 'outage' on anything that impacts the customer or their ability to get their job done. They will expect suppliers to have a similarly high level of response and to be able to service their needs and rapidly resolve any issues.

Ethical and environmental considerations

Another aspect in terms of removing risk from the supply chain process is to ensure that you are aligned with the kind of ethical and environmental considerations that a major retail chain would expect.

In particular, if you are selling a product to retailers they would expect you to have reams of documentation to prove that the factories you use have been audited to an acceptable standard and are not, for instance, known to use child labour. Retailers have been hurt in the past by press and media coverage of suspected involvement with suppliers that use child labour. Consumers who see and hear this kind of news often boycott those retailers and obviously sales are massively impacted. In several cases it has later been proven that the allegations were false, that no child labour was involved. That said, a press apology can never compensate for the lost sales or the long-term damage done to consumer perception of that retail brand. As a result of such things, retailers are understandably concerned about the factories used by their suppliers and will require evidence of factory audits to protect themselves and to prove they did everything possible to avoid being associated with unethical manufacturing processes.

When I work with clients who use factories overseas to make their products, or who employ offshore developers where they have a service proposition, I advise that they secure the services of an expert in global sourcing and supplier management. This kind of consultant will be invaluable to your business success; they will be able to arrange audits to ensure that all parties are compliant with the kind of exacting standards a retailer would expect *and* they will be able to provide you with all the reports and documentation you'd need to demonstrate this when asked to do so by a retailer.

Engaging expert services for key areas that are beyond your own expertise is fundamental to your ability to create and grow your business, as we discussed in Chapter 3 on people. It's that wider team which make your business look credible. By working with a global sourcing and supplier management expert you will be able to show retailers how serious you are about being a quality supplier to them, removing any doubt they may have had that trading with you was a risk.

The next thing to consider, now you know that you can fulfil orders, is how you will pay for them and, most importantly, when you'll be paid.

Managing cash

Retailers have historically traded with suppliers that accept lengthy payment terms; terms of 90 days from receipt of invoice, or worse, from the delivery of goods, are not unusual. While some are a little more flexible, most expect their suppliers to accept these terms.

Clearly, for a small business, managing what might be the biggest order you've ever had to deal with to date, accepting payment terms that extend to 90 days beyond delivery could be enough to dry up your cash flow completely. Of course, without cash flow you risk insolvency. When you've got your own suppliers to pay, who may be unwilling to offer you such extended credit terms due to the fact you are a small business, you'll find that you're stuck between a rock and a hard place. There are some strategies that you can use to manage the issue of cash flow and payment terms. We'll explore these next. Of course, in Chapter 9 on negotiation we'll also look at ways that you might be able to agree more favourable terms with a retail buyer. However, as that may not be an area where a buyer has authority to concede, you do need to be prepared to cover the gap in your cash flow.

Securing funding

Most small businesses find that they need to explore financing options to support their growth, and those that sell to retailers particularly so.

There are several options available for funding, each with pros and cons. Figure 6.2 lists a few of the more common routes to securing funding – this is by no means an exhaustive list but should get you thinking about what options might be available to you.

FIGURE 6.2 Options for securing funding

Funding option	Pros	Cons
Bank business loan	You can plan for the costs as this will be typically structured on a repayment basis, over a timeframe, with a monthly payback. You can always pay back more swiftly if you choose. If you have a clear order/contract from a retail client then you should have little trouble getting a bank to provide you lending against that; in fact, some have special products created specifically to help with the 'financial supply chain' for businesses that sell to retailers and other corporations with long payment terms.	It can be difficult to secure funding without a very solid business case. Many banks are still reluctant to lend to small businesses. Interest rates can be high compared to other sources of finance.
Bank business overdraft	If you have a business account you may be entitled to an overdraft. If so, this is a pre-approved, flexible option that requires no effort to dip into.	Interest rates and other charges can make overdrafts expensive if they are used for more than a month or so. Not a long-term option and possibly also not an adequate amount of finance to cash-flow a major retailer's order value.
Investor loan	A good alternative to a bank, particularly as there are lots of investors who will happily lend you money when you have the security of a retailer order. If it's just a loan it can be quickly put in place, and as investors don't get a good return on their cash from a bank they will consider a short-term loan with a guaranteed return to be a relatively low-risk option if you have that retailer order.	They may want to achieve a relatively high interest rate to get a good return. They may favour an equity share, which we explore on page 120.

FIGURE 6.2   *continued*

Funding option	Pros	Cons
Investor equity share	If you want a successful, wealthy co-owner in your business then this is a great route to secure funding. When you have an investor with an equity share, they will be eager to see you achieve your business goals. You may get their advice and support included in the deal, as the better your business performs, the safer their investment will be and the higher their return on investment will be.	It does take time to structure an investment agreement and for the investor to complete 'due diligence' (a detailed investigation into you, your business, finances, projections etc). They may want to give you the money but you might not want to give the proportion of ownership they are after. If you don't want to give up any part of the business then obviously this is not the route for you.
Personal loans	Often a quick source of finance. You can look at smaller sums on an unsecured loan or larger sums on a mortgage drawdown (if you have equity in your property). The benefit is, of course, that there is no bank or investor involved, no business case to present, so you can just get on with it!	This is entirely your personal risk. Availability of secured loans will depend on whether you have equity in your property, and, as a business owner, if a bank will lend to you (often business owners are classified as a higher risk than employees). Personal loan interest rates can be high.
Family loans	Great *if* you have family with money to invest in you!	You have all the same issues as you have with an investor *and* the added worry of family relationships. Best avoided unless your family member is absolutely clear about the risks and the reward.
Business grants	Free money!	Difficult to secure, takes a long time, may not be adequate to cover your needs.

While there are drawbacks, as with all financing options, I do still think that one of the best routes for businesses which have *very* bold growth plans is to secure an investor. Neil Westwood from Magic Whiteboard did just that when he approached the TV show *Dragon's Den*. There are other routes – I've previously mentioned Angels Den and a number of my clients have had success in securing investment (both loans and equity-based arrangements) through this approach.

The benefit of working with an external investor is, of course, their knowledge, expertise and network. They will have a vested interest in your business achieving its growth plan – their investment depends upon it! It can be exhausting seeking funding, pitching the business plan to investors, negotiating the terms, but those who have ambitious plans recognize that the financial support of an external party may be the best way for them to realize those plans.

One key consideration when securing investment, particularly when it is for an equity share rather than a loan, is to demonstrate that you have protected your brand and your intellectual property. This, of course, is fundamental to your scalability as the business will be unable to scale if its offer has been copied, replicated and the market saturated. With that in mind, the last part of this chapter is focused on what you need to be considering when it comes to protecting your brand and intellectual property.

Protecting your brand

As soon as your brand and ideas are in the public domain they are at risk of being copied or replicated. The better your idea, the more likely it is that this will be attempted. There are only so many things you can do to protect your brand or intellectual property and usually this involves spending a fairly considerable sum with a specialist intellectual property lawyer. Still, if you want to sell to retail, avoid being copied and create a valuable business, this is something that you need to consider seriously.

Retailers have earned a bad reputation for taking ideas and product prototypes from other businesses, perhaps things they've seen at trade shows or had presented to them face to face, and using those ideas to develop a similar range of own-brand products or a similar capability. Here is what you have to remember: retail buyers are not evil! They are not specifically trying to take advantage of creative entrepreneurs and steal ideas. They are driven by commercial objectives, so if they like your product and are pressed by a senior manager to investigate higher-margin options it is only natural that they would look at the costs/complexity of developing a similar product in-house. As a smaller, unknown business there are really only two ways you can avoid this. One is to have a great brand story – to position your product as the one everyone wants. Think about Apple; when MP3 players were new to the market, a consumer could buy one from any brand as well as the retailer's own-brand items. Prices for own-brand items were really favourable and at the end of the day it was an MP3 player, it did exactly the same job... but it wasn't an iPod. iPods quickly dominated the MP3 market; wherever you looked people had them – they began to appear in various colours, sizes, with different storage capabilities. After the iPod arrived, no other MP3 player really got noticed. If you can do that with your brand, copycats don't matter. I would, however, advise a two-pronged attack, making sure that your brand is not only the most desirable, the one everyone wants, but also ensuring that you are covered on the second option. The second option is to be legally protected against copycat behaviour.

There are different types of legal protection for brands and intellectual property, and it varies by country too. In the UK there is the Intellectual Property Office – a great source of advice and insight. You can look at options that include:

- A trademark: this is something that can help people to identify your brand, products or services and it enables them to separate you from your competition. It can be just words, a logo/image or a combination of both. Dr Jonathan Elms at the Institute for Retail Studies is quoted on the UK Intellectual Property Office website saying: 'No matter what market place you operate in; no matter the size and scope of your firm;

a registered trade mark is simply a must for your business. It will serve to protect, differentiate and add value to what you do – and therefore make your business stand out in the crowd.'

- Copyright: you can apply copyright to any type of content you create that can be copied with ease. You need permission to reproduce copyright-protected materials. Things that are protected by copyright include published photographs, written work, music, art and design. Copyright is automatically applied when something is published; you don't have to apply for it. Copyright doesn't protect any concepts or ideas, only the finished work.

- A patent: this is a form of protection that only applies to *new* inventions. You definitely need to seek advice on this, as when you register a patent you need to include all the mechanics and capabilities of your invention – how it works, what it does, how it does it, what it's made of, how it's made... the point being to give the inventor protection that would mean other parties could be prevented from doing anything that encroached on the patent without permission. Apple has been exceptionally foresighted in this area, having patented a whole host of usability and user interface developments for the iPhone and specifically the iOS operating system, which means that other developers of smartphone operating systems, such as Google Android, have been in legal wranglings over the nuances of the user interface they have developed as it has been accused of encroaching on Apple's patents.

- Design rights: this is a complex area in the UK as there are rights for both registered and unregistered designs. Again, one for your expert lawyer to assess for you. There are strict criteria about what can and what cannot be protected. Design rights apply to an object's, or part of an object's, overall visual appearance. To be awarded any form of protection it has to be new and individual, not like anything else.

Intellectual property is a very specialist area of law. I've listed some of the most likely protection options that may be relevant to a business selling to retailers. If your business has unique inventions or developments you should seek to protect those with some urgency in order to protect the intrinsic value of the business. Assigning a budget to get protection for your intellectual property or brand should be on your priority list. Linking back to the earlier point about investment, protected rights will certainly be attractive to investors should you wish to approach them for funding.

Wrapping up

In this chapter we have considered what ingredients need to be in place to enable you to upscale your business operations. We have covered:

- what scalability actually means and how to develop a robust and repeatable platform for your business;
- managing the supply chain, mitigating risks;
- managing cash flow and options for securing funding;
- protection of your intellectual property to avoid copycats and to add value.

Part Two: Plan Big – summing up

In this part we've been focusing on what you need to plan for in order to grow your business, considering your market, which is made up of the customer and the competition, as well as reviewing the scalability of your business operations.

As a result of the three chapters in this part you should have a clear action plan, based on detailed research and analysis, about who your ideal customers are, how you compare to the competition, and how you can deliver a reliable and consistent supply of goods (or services) to your customers when they place their business with you.

We have defined:

1   your ideal or target customer (mindful of both the end consumer and the retail buyer);

2   your competitive landscape, who they are, what they offer, how you differentiate;

3   how you will upscale your business to meet the demands of your customers.

So you've got it all planned out. We're going to wrap up this part on Plan Big with a simple checklist (Figure 6.3) for you to go through to make sure that you've covered all the groundwork to avoid being caught out when it's pitch time.

This checklist is also available for download, if you prefer, via **www.retailchampion.co.uk/selling-to-retailers/resources**.

continued on page 128

FIGURE 6.3 Part Two checklist

Area	Ingredient	Complete? (yes/no)	Action to address (if any)	Cost implications?	Priority (H/M/L)	Target date to complete
Customer	Ensuring you have a clear understanding of end user					
Customer	Ensuring you have a clear understanding of the buyer and what influences them					
Customer	Creating a prioritized target list of ideal buyers, including the reasons why they are ideal					
Customer	Getting clarity on your pricing strategy and how this marries up to positioning					
Competition	Completing an analysis of the competition					

Competition	Developing processes to stay abreast of competitor developments and new entrants				
Scalability	Ensuring your internal processes and systems are robust and repeatable				
Scalability	Getting a clear view of the constraints of your supply chain				
Scalability	Confirming that you can access sources of funding, if required, to manage cash flow in the growth phase				
Scalability	Seeking to protect your intellectual property				

Part Two: Plan Big – summing up   *continued*

Now you've completed the checklist, the onus is on you to actually implement the actions to address the gaps.

PART THREE
Pitch Big

In Part Two we did a great deal of groundwork in order to have the information we need for this part:

- We've identified which buyers to approach and we've got some basic information about them.
- We know how to differentiate ourselves effectively from the competition.
- We have confidence in our ability to support the demand of a major retail client.

This will all be very useful content for us to use when developing and delivering our pitch.

In this part we'll be covering a further three chapters, focusing on the sale itself and exploring:

- what preparation is required to ensure you are ready to present to a potential customer by drawing together much of the work you've done in Part Two and really focusing on your top retailer target customers;
- how to go about the end-to-end process of selling your product or service to the retailer, from first point of contact, to follow-up, and to getting the initial interest confirmed;
- then, and following a confirmation of initial interest, how to deal with the inevitable negotiations in order to achieve a win–win outcome and the basis of a quality, long-term retailer–supplier relationship.

At the end of this part we'll recap on the key components of 'Pitch Big', with a checklist for you to go through to make sure you've got all the necessary ingredients in place.

Preparation

07

Introduction

In this chapter we'll be looking at all the preparation you need to do for your pitch. We will look at the steps that are required as part of the pre-sales preparation, including:

- researching the retailer in more detail, developing a clear and detailed understanding of what will really matter to the specific retail buyer;

- from this research, determining why this retailer needs your product or service, making some educated guesses as to how it supports them in delivering on their business objectives;

- using what you know to prepare a detailed proposal that will include all of the relevant financial information as well as any other pertinent information about your offer;

- designing your sales presentation, rehearsing it with others and getting their feedback and critique, enabling you to finesse it in readiness to take it in front of a potential new customer.

In the context of this entire part, Pitch Big, your preparation will be the most valuable element. The selling process should become relatively easy if you've done a good job of preparation. Negotiation is about getting an optimal outcome for both parties once an agreement in principle to buy has been given by the retailer. Before you can reach the sales presentation or indeed the negotiation, you'll have to have done the preparation, so let's get started!

Developing a detailed understanding of each retailer uniquely

In the chapter about customers you'll have worked towards a far better understanding of who they are and why. Now we need to look at a list of your top 10 target retailers, to determine who are most important to you and why. This won't only be to do with sales, it will also be to do with which retail brands are most closely aligned to yours – which brands give your product the best exposure and best placement in terms of your target end user and your positioning.

Spend some time thinking this through, and once you are clear as to who your 10 most ideal target retailers are, you need to prioritize them. It may take a few attempts, shuffling them around on your list until you are happy. You should have the most important at position number 1 and the least important (of your top 10) at position number 10. Obviously, as these are your top 10 they are *all* important but it will be a valuable exercise to challenge yourself and ensure that you create this prioritized list, as then you'll have also clarified your thinking as to *why* a specific retailer is so important to you, which will help you to focus on that reason when it comes to developing the pitch.

When starting your first-ever sales process I'd urge you to start with number 10 on the list. While obviously still very important to you, so you'll still make a great deal of effort to get it right (this is not one you want to lose), they're not as critical as number 1. While it would be disappointing if you didn't come away with a deal from your number 10, what this target will give you, at the very least, is a list of lessons learnt that you can apply to number 9. You may still get an open door, for example 'give us a call in six months', if you did a good job, they liked you, but the timing wasn't quite right. Don't forget that with any target that doesn't result in a deal you can always ask for a call/1-2-1 with the buyer for some specific feedback. People don't tend to be obnoxious just for the sake of it – chances are that as long as you did a quality presentation the buyer will respect you enough as a business person to give you some of their time and to provide you with feedback. You can learn a huge amount of valuable insight from a target that says 'no' to you. Don't miss the opportunity to get as much feedback as possible. The reason I mention this now, when technically an unsuccessful pitch is the outcome of Chapter 9 on negotiation, is because you would need to incorporate all those lessons learnt into any future preparation.

Imagine how much more confident and well prepared you'd be when approaching target number 9 if you've been able to use and leverage the lessons learnt and feedback from number 10. Every step through your list of targets helps you to finesse your approach, refining what works well, what retailers responded to, avoiding what they didn't. Part of the preparation for each and every pitch (after the very first) *must* be an analysis and appraisal of the previous pitch.

Emma Wimhurst explained how much she learnt from her very first pitch to New Look:

My first meeting was with New Look, I called them up and they agreed to see me. I had a vision that I'd sell them a full cosmetics fixture, with various vibrant products and colour ways. It didn't go to plan. They did agree to buy, but only nail polish. Initially I was quite disappointed – it wasn't what I envisaged. However, I learnt a huge amount – the biggest lesson was to use my ears and mouth in the proportion that they were given to me: listen with two ears, talk with one mouth! At that time the New Look buyer knew their customer better than I did, they liked my ideas, and me, enough to trial it with nail polish. As a result of the trial, which was a sell-out success, New Look had tested and proved the concept I had presented. They requested that we upscale production and supply them with sufficient product for further roll-out. It went from there, a step at a time. Looking back, in spite of the initial disappointment of not implementing the full cosmetics fixture, this was the best thing that could have happened. It taught me how to approach future presentations to retailers, by putting myself in their shoes and in the shoes of their customer. I was now better equipped to sell an initial trial with the plan for a subsequent roll-out, subject to success. This was far more palatable to the retailers. Had I got what I envisaged at the outset with New Look I might never have learnt to adopt this 'trial-to-roll-out' approach and maybe would not have been as lucky with other retailers as I was with New Look.

If the New Look buyer had dismissed Emma at the first meeting rather than offering a trial, she would not have learnt that valuable lesson; although if she had requested feedback, she might have uncovered the reasons why her proposal wasn't accepted. If the buyer had accepted the proposal full-scale Emma also would not have learnt the step-by-step approach; again, something that was an invaluable lesson for future pitches with major retail targets.

The other thing Emma learnt was to consider each customer uniquely – she comments that New Look knew their customer far better than she did, they knew that a nail polish placed at the point of sale, where they queued to pay, was an impulse purchase – low cost and requiring little thought. Perfect for the New Look ideal customer who might have overlooked an entire cosmetics counter because that's not what they'd necessarily have expected to find in New Look at that time.

Emma absolutely believes that her success was based on really knowing the retailer's customer; the fact that her team were *so* in tune with each of her target retailers' customer groups that they might have known them better than the retailers did themselves. Before any presentation that Diva delivered, Emma and her team did a huge amount of analysis and research into the needs and wants of each specific retailer's customer. When they did get in front of a client, they were able not only to present the product in a way which made it compelling to the buyer, but they were also able to explain all the reasoning as to why this product was perfect for that retailer's customer group, backed up with insights and analysis of sale volumes, market need etc that proved to the retailer that the product Emma's team presented was a 'safe bet'.

So, I hope Emma's story illustrates what we need to do next. Once we've got that prioritized list of retailer targets we need to take each of them, one by one, and develop a far more detailed understanding of their business.

Now we will explore the kind of information you really need to know, why you need to know it, and where you can find it. Figure 7.1 lists a number of key areas that you need to consider. You need to go through this process of research and investigation into each and every retailer that you plan to approach.

FIGURE 7.1 What you need to know about each and every target retail customer

The kind of things you need to know	Why you need to know it	Where you can find it out
Financials, annual reports. From these you should get an understanding of key retail commercial data such as: – number of stores; – channels/markets; – sales, by category if available; – margin achieved/ expected; – profit per square foot; – past 3–5 years' financial performance across key metrics (sales, return on space, margin etc).	As a minimum you need to know that this is a customer who can pay your invoices – just because they are big doesn't mean they're not as exposed to difficulties as every other business. Do your checks to make sure that if you supply them you will get paid. In addition, you need to understand their current trading dynamic – margin performance, profit per square foot (if disclosed) and what the trend has been over recent years (improving or declining). This will help you understand how your offer can help the retailer improve, delivering a positive impact on their key financial metrics.	There is a great deal of data available, free of charge, online. Most retailers, and particularly those who are public companies, publish their annual reports on their own website. These tend to include all the key financial data as well as an overview about their strategy and direction – this is always the best place to start. If you don't find what you need, there is nothing to stop you phoning the head office and asking if they can send you a printed copy of their annual report. Privately held companies may not publish this information widely, but most of the larger retailers do. Another resource, particularly useful to those in the UK, is 'Retail Week Knowledge Bank' – a repository of *all* key data, by retailer, including all press releases and coverage. It's available to all those who subscribe to the *Retail Week* publication. Similar tools are available, almost all at a cost, so your best bet is to start with what you can discover from reputable, free online sources.

FIGURE 7.1 *continued*

The kind of things you need to know	Why you need to know it	Where you can find it out
The key people, decision makers, influencers on the process of a retailer deciding to buy from you: – buying director; – commercial director. For services, the director on whom your service has most impact in the business and potentially the director whose budget would pay for any implementation, as these are not necessarily the same function: – CEO/MD; – COO/Finance.	You need to know a bit about who you are dealing with, what their background is etc. Remember, big organizations can have a lot of internal politics; you need to ensure you speak to all of the right people and are inclusive, to avoid alienating someone. You can also identify if you have any common connections with the retailer contacts – a great ice-breaker is to mention a mutual friend/colleague – as long as you're confident that the person you mention is well regarded; the last thing you want to do is mention someone they dislike! In most retailers *all* buying decisions, for both products and services, are made by a team, not by an individual, so make sure you are identifying people at all levels – both decision makers and influencers.	I have personally found the online network LinkedIn to be absolutely essential when I've been researching 'who's who' in major retailers. Often a Google search for 'buying director of [Retailer]' will give you some names that you can then take to LinkedIn to find out more. Other options include annual reports and press coverage – often key individuals are named. Even the retailer's website may include pages about key personnel. The other option is to buy a data set – there are various organizations that sell marketing data that can include all kinds of other useful insights – but be careful, make sure you buy from a reputable source as out-of-date data is useless and you will be wasting your money. Finally, you could always call Reception and simply ask 'who is head of buying for XYZ?'

FIGURE 7.1 *continued*

The kind of things you need to know	Why you need to know it	Where you can find it out
Their current strategy and direction, their goal, mission and positioning.	When you know details of where the business is going, what they stand for and how they are positioned, it gives you the ability to explain to the retailer, in your presentation, why you are a good fit for them. You can build rapport on an interpersonal level as well as prove why you are a great strategic partner for a retailer if you can highlight synergies where your own strategy, mission or positioning align to theirs. You will also discover key 'hooks' that you can include in your pitch. For example, if a retailer states that they wish to expand into new markets and you offer a software solution that enables them to sell in multi-language and multi-currency (and they currently can't do that), then of course you have the reason why they need to be speaking to you, because what you offer enables them to meet their aims.	You can find the vast majority of this information on the retailers' own websites and certainly in their annual reports. You might find comments about strategy or future direction in press coverage as well, but make sure the press you reference is reputable and that the quoted sources are credible, otherwise you may be using erroneous information for the basis of your pitch.

FIGURE 7.1   *continued*

The kind of things you need to know	Why you need to know it	Where you can find it out
Any recent news features or press releases.	As touched on earlier, news features can be a source of information about who's who as well as future strategy and direction.	Again for this I'd turn to Google, searching in 'News' for any mention of the retailer's name. I'd also review their own website – there is often a press page where recent releases are published.
	Press releases, especially those published by the retailer about their business, give you an insight into what they want to be made public knowledge about their organization. This gives you an insight into how they want to influence consumer opinion, and will back up (or maybe contradict) the information you have about their strategy, direction, positioning etc.	It may well be worth paying for a subscription to some of the key trade press as you'll often be able to access more information about the retailer's business from the trade press than you can from even the most reputable consumer press.
Their customer.	You *must* know their customer – they are the people who will be buying *your* product if you are a product supplier. You need do what Emma did and demonstrate exactly what it is about your product that their customer will want, why they should buy from you.	You can't get this information in a structured format; you have to work it out – they're not going to make it public, that would be giving too much away to their own competitors.
		Visit stores, at different times of day, make a mental note of who the people are that are spending money. Begin to build up a really clear image of who this retailer's ideal customer is from what you see in-store.

FIGURE 7.1 *continued*

The kind of things you need to know	Why you need to know it	Where you can find it out
	If you are providing services you still should have a detailed understanding of the customer – it's who the retailer is in business to serve, it's where they derive their revenue from. As mentioned previously, even as a services supplier, when it comes to your pitch you should be identifying *how* the retailer will be better able to serve their customer (directly or indirectly) as a result of your support. Don't assume that the retailer won't expect you to understand their customer – they will.	Review their product ranges, pricing, positioning – you should be able to work out who they are trying to attract – you will have a view in any case, the fact you'd identified with a retailer and included them on your top 10 target list says that you have a 'feeling' (based on experience or prior research) that this retailer is likely to be serving the right kind of customers for you to sell to (if you are a product supplier), *or*, if you are a services supplier, you will have had a similar 'gut feel' as to who the retailers are who would most likely respond to what you offer, based on research, observation or on your own experience of them.
What ranges they sell, and how what you offer may either supplement existing ranges, add a new range, or, in the case of services, enable ranges to be better managed.	Product suppliers need to know this as a priority, obviously, to be able to determine how their product fits alongside the current offer – is it entirely new (as cosmetics were in New Look) or is it an extension of what's already on sale?	You can get this information from visiting stores or reviewing their e-commerce sites. It's readily available as obviously it has to be presented for sale to customers.

FIGURE 7.1   *continued*

The kind of things you need to know	Why you need to know it	Where you can find it out
	Service suppliers need to know this by way of background at the very least. However, many retailers start with trials of new products *and* services – as in Emma's experience – so it would help if you had in mind an approach to a trial of your services, eg 'how about we prove the concept on menswear and if successful we can roll out to women's wear later in the year'. You would not be in a position to engage in those conversations if you had not really understood their category mix and offer.	

This research helps you begin to build a picture as to the state of the retail business that you hope to sell to. Now we need to consider how you can hook your product offering or service proposition into that information in order to gather together the 'story' you need for the pitch.

Why does this client really *need* your offer?

With all that research in mind, you need to connect your knowledge of the retail business to all the key features, benefits and opportunities of your product or service. Using your insights and your competitor analysis you can begin to build up a story to use in your presentation to the buyer that explains how your product or service supports their strategy or addresses gaps.

Reflecting on each of the elements once again, Figure 7.2 explores what you might be able to present to connect into each of the key areas.

FIGURE 7.2 How to connect your product/service to the key information about your target retail customer

What you need to know	How your product/service ties into this
Financials, annual reports. From these you should get an understanding of key retail commercial data such as: – number of stores; – channels/markets; – sales, by category if available; – margin achieved/expected; – profit per square foot; – past 3–5 years' financial performance across key metrics (sales, return on space, margin etc).	In your proposal/presentation or pitch you can touch on how, by buying into your offering, you help them deliver on key financials. For products, that may be about increasing margin, return on space or basket size. It may be about attracting new customers or increasing frequency of visit. All metrics that increase sales. If you are selling a service then, depending on what you offer, you need to tie into any metrics that either increase sales/margin or reduce costs, eg stock planning that improves availability of product on shelf actually could increase the overall capital tied up in stock *but* if you demonstrate that in fact it increases full-price sales, by reducing overstocks in some locations and out-of-stocks in others, then you will show how your solution can increase margin and customer satisfaction by having product available when customers attempt to purchase it. If you focus on the retailer's key financials, in particular where some key metric has been in a negative trend or static (as opposed to a positive trend), you can mention how your particular proposal would support the business in delivering improvement in these areas. The key is to leverage your knowledge and understanding of the retailer's business performance to highlight how working with you could enable them to make a positive difference and achieve the business objectives.

FIGURE 7.2   *continued*

What you need to know	How your product/service ties into this
The key people, decision makers, influencers on the process of a retailer deciding to buy from you: – buying director; – commercial director. For services, the director on whom your service has most impact in the business and potentially the director whose budget would pay for any implementation, as these are not necessarily the same function: – CEO/MD; – COO/Finance.	It's obvious really when you think about it – you need to know who you need to convince. It's good to have an 'internal champion' who really wants the business to work with you, someone who believes in what you offer and understands your value add. You also need to ensure you've built relationships with all those who are not only making the decisions but potentially those who could scupper them! When you write your proposal or deliver a presentation, make sure you've got something included for all interested parties. You need to ensure that each understands the benefit of what you offer to them – in their job, in delivering their personal objectives and in supporting the business as a whole.
Their current strategy and direction, their goal, mission and positioning.	Similar to understanding their financials, if you are aware of what statement of direction they have made you will be able to demonstrate how your offer enables them to achieve that more rapidly.
Any recent news features or press releases.	As per the above items, if you have noticed any comment or reviews that demonstrate why the retailer needs your product or service you can reference those; however, as mentioned earlier, make sure the news is from a credible source!
Their customer.	In any retail business they are the most important people to consider. You need to really understand, and be able to demonstrate with analysis, research or case studies, exactly how your offering enhances the shopping experience, directly or indirectly, for the retailer's customer.

FIGURE 7.2 *continued*

What you need to know	How your product/service ties into this
	If you sell a product you need to prove that it is something that their customer would want, that it complements the existing range, and offers choice.
	If you sell a service you need to show how, as a result of the retailer buying your services, they will be able to deliver a better, more efficient service to their customer.
	If what you offer is merely about increasing profitability, you can still reference the customer – the shareholders of a business can be described as internal customers, so by increasing profit you increase shareholder value. You also allow the business an opportunity to invest in developments – thus even services which initially appear to not touch on the customer do ultimately benefit the customer by helping a retailer be sustainable, profitable and able to reinvest in their customer experience.
What ranges they sell, and how what you offer may either supplement existing ranges, add a new range or, in the case of services, enable ranges to be better managed.	Obviously retailers need to present products to customers, and therefore if you sell a product you need to prove how it is beneficial to the retailer.
	Bringing in a new product can be costly – in fact some retailers charge new suppliers a 'listing fee' to help cover their admin and operational costs. The retailer is unlikely to just have a gap on a shelf or on the shop floor ready for your item – they need to make space. What should come off sale to make way for you, and why? If you can't demonstrate how your product adds more value – through higher margins, greater volume or a better alignment to the core customer – then a retailer won't be delisting something else to make a gap for you.

FIGURE 7.2   *continued*

What you need to know	How your product/service ties into this
	If you sell services, as touched on above, you need to focus on how your offering enables the retailer to better manage the product – by saving time, reducing cost, giving better visibility of information – in the same way as any value-adding solution can be connected to a customer benefit, it can also be connected to a product benefit. For example, by implementing a new intranet solution, stores won't need to call buying teams with enquiries, rather they can look up information or post a question. This means less disruption for the teams, allowing them to focus on core tasks, reducing head count required for managing calls from stores by an equivalent of ½ FTE per category (FTE stands for full-time equivalent, it's a way of measuring resources). This is the kind of business statement that further proves your understanding of a retailer's priorities and pressures. It's that kind of connection to core activities (selling product to customers) that will ensure your proposal or pitch gets the attention it deserves.

So now that we've walked through some ideas about how to connect your offer to the key considerations, we're going to look at the more interpersonal elements of the buyer–seller relationship.

What is the benefit to the buyer of buying from you?

Part of explaining why the client really needs your offer is not only to focus on the business but to focus on the buyer as an individual. We touched on this in Chapter 4. As we said, not only do people buy from people, but retail buyers are constantly being approached with ideas from entrepreneurs, so you need to stand out. If the buyer doesn't remember you or doesn't want to forge a relationship with you, it won't matter how good the product or service is, or how well it supports the business in achieving its aims; if the buyer rejects you there will be little more you can do.

From the outset you need to make it quite clear that you're not just looking for a quick buck by selling your product or service, you are actually going to be someone they can rely on not only to meet the contract demands but to make their job easier. You need to be 'on their side' and develop a relationship of trust so that they can champion your proposal internally through the inevitable layers of sign-off.

Again, this is something Emma Wimhurst learnt when she was growing Diva Cosmetics, and I would go as far as to say that this is possibly one of the key reasons why Emma enjoyed such rapid growth and achieved the level of success that she did. Emma had tried to employ a sales person, but it wasn't working out. She realized that as a small business it was her passion, her knowledge and her expertise that made the difference when it came to forging relationships with buyers in the early stages. Much as she'd wanted to distance herself from the sales process, to maintain the position of managing director, she realized that as a small business – and to build relationships of trust from the outset – the retailer needed to meet her in person. Once trust was established through consistently delivering on promises, Emma was able to delegate the account management to one of her team, but that first contact needed to be between Emma and the buyer. Emma said:

> When in front of the buyer each and every presentation was 100 per cent tailored to them, I never ever gave the same presentation to two retailers. I made sure that I knew each retailer's positioning, their point of difference, and so I was able to tailor what was presented to really resonate with them. Treating each retailer, and each buyer, uniquely really made the difference. Of course I was well prepared too, I knew all the financial details about each retailer, I'd researched everything I could about them. Before I even quit my day job I'd analysed the market, identified a need and worked out who my ideal retailers would be.

I knew I needed them to trust in me and the ability of my team to deliver. I was also aware that should I win a contract I could be penalized for failure, so I was always completely open and honest, I knew what we could and could not deliver and all the associated cost implications. If I'd not been prepared and not developed a trust relationship with the buyer I don't think they'd have given Diva a chance.

So, reflecting on everything you've learnt about the retailer, you need to make sure that you do as Emma did – secure the trust of the buyer – and while you can only achieve that face to face, when you are in the process of selling, you can prepare for that before you even contact them to request a meeting. Being armed with all the facts and information, all the knowledge and insight, will give you far greater confidence in the selling process, will enable you to answer difficult questions accurately and, as a result, all the hard work done in preparation should make the difference between a buyer trusting you, or not.

In the latter part of this chapter we're going to look at what needs to be included in your proposal or presentation and how to get ready to present. That, of course, will conclude preparation, because once you are ready to present you can start to sell.

What you need to include in your proposal or presentation

We've already touched on most of what you need to cover; however, there is a difference between a neatly presented pack as a leave-behind and the presentation you deliver in person. Your proposal may well be sent ahead of a meeting, in order to secure a meeting, or left as supplementary materials following a meeting. In each case, it needs to contain the five items listed below (although it's up to you and your style as to how you structure these). If you have no experience of either creating or receiving a professional proposal in your career, it would be worth either getting hold of some as examples, or seeking expert advice to help you get this right.

Proposal contents

1 Executive summary – a maximum of two sides of A4 that states what the rest of the document details; it's the snapshot view. If a senior manager read this page, and then checked with their team that you lived up to the statements made, they should feel confident to give their team the nod of approval based on the content in this section alone. It's important that they don't need to wade through a detailed document; they often won't as they don't have time.

2 Background and Introduction – a brief history of how you have come to be providing the proposal, a summary of the communications you have had thus far, and with whom. Also a brief introduction to your company and to what will be included within the balance of the document.

3 Core proposal – the content that articulates what you propose and why. This should include:

   a details of costs;

   b timescales;

   c any known constraints;

   d preferred mode of engagement;

   e details of the key contact person.

4 Supplementary information – here you could back up claims with any relevant market analysis, research, white papers, information about your business, credentials, accreditations, key personnel, testimonials, case studies, press coverage – in fact you can outline *anything* that really backs up your proposal.

   – However, this is still the summary, the overview, so you can mention that you have X, Y, Z audits on factories etc *but* don't include the whole thing here. You can attach it as an appendix or make it available on request.

5 Next steps – outline your expectations with regard to next steps and include the contact details once again, including e-mail, web address, postal address, phone number.

So that's a proposal sorted out – how you use it is up to you and we'll explore the actual sales process in the next chapter. Now you need to prepare yourself for a presentation; if you secure a formal meeting you'll be expected to present, possibly to a wider audience than the person you've initially had contact with. You'll be compared to every other supplier they've ever seen – including global mega-brands – so it needs to be good! Let's look at what's expected now.

Getting ready to present

The last step in preparation is getting your presentation pulled together and being ready to present. Chances are your sales process will involve you being invited in to do a formal presentation to the team involved in the buying decision. If you sell services you may have to present to several groups; for product suppliers it is usually various members of the category team.

It's normal practice to use PowerPoint or a similar tool as a visual aid, and so you need to lift all the most compelling points from your proposal to create a presentation that effectively tells the audience the 'story' from the proposal in a succinct and engaging manner. You need to include the key messages that we identified when we were looking at why this retailer *needs* your product or service, and make sure that the visual aid supports what you are saying as you present. You may find that you get nervous before a presentation – that's normal. If you need to seek some external help to ensure you've got well-polished presentation skills, it will be money well spent as you have really only got one chance to get this right when you are live in front of a buyer.

Once you have your presentation structured, the slides created and the patter (what you will say) in mind, you need to practise it. You can do this either to a video camera (a really useful way for you to see how you present and self-critique) or to an audience made up of people you trust who will give you brutally honest feedback.

Quite often I ask clients to present to me before they go in to see a retailer, and I ask all those dreadful questions, the type that brings beads of sweat to your brow! Since 1996 I've been employed (either directly or as a consultant) by retailers as part of a buying team or a project team with the remit specifically to ask those difficult questions. We weren't doing it to distress the potential future supplier, we really did need those answers – often the difficult, testing questions were the ones that actually differentiated two suppliers, and we'd choose to work with the supplier who could achieve a certain supply chain target or deliver a specific systems capability. Now I leverage that insight, into what the supplier can sometimes see as a very brutal round of quick-fire questions, for the benefit of my clients. If their pitch breaks down in a rehearsal, with just me and a few of their team in the room, we have time to go over each of the 'sticky' points and work out what the answers need to be to address any objections or query, satisfying the retailer so that we can move on with the presentation. All too often when I've been on the retailer side I've seen a pitch completely derailed because the supplier got stuck on a question. When this happens, their whole flow is thrown out, their credibility comes into question, and the chance of them finishing the pitch is minimal. We'd usually tell them to stop, go away, and come back only when they felt able to give us a decent response to our issue. Occasionally we'd 'park' the issue, agree to put it to one side with the intent to come back to it later. In reality we'd often lost confidence in the supplier at that point; the rest of the presentation was being over-scrutinized and the best answer in the world to the parked issue was unlikely ever to put them back into a strong position in the eyes of the decision-making team. As a buying team we were usually under huge time pressures, needing to get to a quick decision and proceed with a supplier to deliver a project. We needed to choose a safe bet, a confident and capable supplier, and that wasn't often one who'd stumbled in their pitch.

So, bearing that in mind, I hope you'll rehearse your presentation and plan answers to all manner of potential objections, questions, requests for more detail etc, to avoid being sent away in disgrace.

Don't despair, though, you can give a confident answer of 'I don't know. Rather than I try to answer that now and not give you the full picture, let me make a note to come back to you with an accurate answer by...' and promise a time. This is very reassuring to the buyer and a good way to put a difficult challenge to the side. It ensures that you can keep moving forward positively. You will have also given the audience confidence that you're not making it all up, you are honest, trustworthy and will not overstate what you don't know. That goes a long way to building trust. The inference here is that should you become a supplier to that retailer you won't overpromise and underdeliver, something that far too many organizations are guilty of. In fact, past supplier failure is probably the main reason why retail buyers do ask so many difficult questions; they've been hurt by supplier failures before and really don't want it to happen again.

Wrapping up

In this chapter we have focused on the preparation required before attempting to sell to a retailer. We have discussed how to:

- research the retailer in detail to better understand what matters to them;
- leverage that insight into the buyer and the retailer to explain why they really do need the product or service;
- put together a comprehensive proposal document;
- develop the presentation to present in the sales meeting.

In the next chapter we'll look at the end-to-end process of selling; this is when it all comes to life and, at last, after all the research, product development, planning and preparation, you can sit face to face with a retailer and share your vision.

Selling

08

Introduction

This chapter brings to life the process of selling, the main purpose of this book! It is about all the actual interactions with your retail buyer, from securing an initial meeting to closing a deal. We'll go from having a well-prepared proposal and presentation to getting confirmation from the retailer of their intent to buy from you, subject to negotiation, which is where we begin Chapter 9. We will cover:

- planning the sales process, determining the steps along the way and what your desired outcome is for each step towards the end goal of commencing negotiations with a retailer;

- getting in front of the decision makers, ensuring you get the opportunity to share your proposition with the right people;

- following up, making sure that you stay in regular contact and keep the sales process moving along.

Having done so much preparation, this should be a relatively comfortable process which you can enter into with confidence.

Planning the outcomes

In any sales process, if you try to close the deal during the first conversation you're doomed to failure, as you're asking a person that you're probably meeting for the first time to buy into the whole concept of what you offer and agree a deal – that's a completely unreasonable request to make of anyone. Imagine how you would feel in such a situation. Rather than jump in, with great enthusiasm, expecting them to buy into your concept in the blink of an eye, you should be taking it a step at a time. To do this you need to plan out the steps along the way, starting with the end in mind. Doing this will enable you to break down the process into the steps that you ideally want to take place, from first point of contact to closing the deal. Then at each point of contact, each step along the way, all you have to do is focus on 'selling' agreement to move to the next step.

It's difficult – you know and love your proposition, and your preparation about this retailer has you all fired up to tell them excitedly why you are the answer to all their prayers. Unfortunately, as the retailer was neither party to the preparation nor do they (yet) share your passion for your proposition, you're going to have to take a deep breath, step back, and take them from their place of relative ignorance about what you offer to being almost as excited about the opportunities as you are!

You need to design your ideal sales process, to include each of the steps along the way, what you want to achieve at each touch point, and what information/confirmation you need from the buyer to have successfully moved on to the next stage.

By way of example, the following outline process would be something you could adapt and work from; each of these steps will be explored in more detail in the remainder of the chapter:

1 **Make the initial contact**: At this stage all you have to do is secure their agreement to have an initial, face-to-face 'exploratory meeting'. You're only selling the concept of spending about an hour with you, over a coffee, so that they can get to know you and get a bit more detail about your offering.

2 **Exploratory meeting**: At this stage you need to learn the details of their preferred buying process. This will enable you to tailor your next steps to fit in with the way that they are most comfortable to move forward. If you are unable to get confirmation of the process from the buyer, you can offer a choice: for example, would they prefer you to put forward a more detailed proposal to read and digest, or would they like you to deliver a presentation to the wider team? Depending on the retailer, and on your preferred style, you may want the next

two steps (submitting a proposal and formal presentation) to be in a different order. Some retailers have additional steps in their process; they like to have an initial proposal, a formal presentation and then a detailed proposal (something they can say 'yes' to and that forms the basis of your scope of engagement and contractual obligations). Other retailers would rather see a couple of presentations, initially to the core team and then, assuming they were happy with the content, to the wider team. They may expect you to leave behind a detailed proposal following a wider team presentation or they may want you to send one in, based on a standard format that they use. Others retailers will have a different process again. The crux is that you understand what's expected of you and work your way through each step to a successful outcome.

3 **Submitting a proposal**: As mentioned above, this step may come later in the process, it may be split (summary proposal, detailed proposal) or it may not even be required. As with all prior steps, you need to ensure that the outcome of this step is the beginning of the next.

4 **Formal presentation**: This may or may not be the last stage, depending on their process. In any formal presentation you are finally selling your expertise, your team and your offering – and the retailer has to believe in everything that they see and hear. It's through this face-to-face engagement with the wider retail team that you have to move from a position of being 'unknown' to most of the audience to a position of being 'known' and, ideally, trusted by them. It is during the face-to-face presentations that you will build rapport with the audience, observe body language, understand team dynamics *and* get all your key points across. With so much to consider simultaneously, unless you have prior expertise of sales presentations from your earlier career, you'll certainly feel the benefit of having done all the preparation and rehearsals. If you are still concerned, I really do think it would be prudent to invest in some specific presentation skills training or sales skills training prior to delivering a face-to-face presentation.

5 Following up: This step is unique in that is should actually follow *all* of the prior steps. For example, if you don't get agreement to move to the next step during the current step then you need to agree when you will call back to follow up and agree a date/timescale for the next actions. Do not underestimate the level of following up and chasing that you need to do to progress. We'll talk through that later.

At the end of the process the final follow-up is probably a 1-2-1 call or meeting with the buyer, as a debriefing. At that stage (if not before) you will secure their confirmation of intent to buy from you, and likely as not enter into the negotiation phase.

These five steps typically form the overall sales process, featuring somewhere along the route from introduction to closing a deal. What we now need to consider is what is involved in each step and how you can actually go about it.

Making the initial contact

In the previous chapter you'll have identified your 'target' and so now we need to make contact. As outlined above, the key is to ensure you *only* aim to get agreement to have an initial exploratory meeting in the first instance. How to do that really effectively is something that writers on sales techniques can help with; whole books are dedicated to selling techniques, so if you want to go into real detail on this aspect (the sales process and selling techniques) then I would recommend looking at a specific text on the topic. In this section we're going to consider some of the key things to watch out for and we'll appraise the different methods that you might be able to use to make contact with a retail buyer in order to secure an exploratory meeting.

The first barrier to be mindful of, and worthy of note, is 'the gate-keeper' – usually a secretary, receptionist or PA. This individual 'protects' your ideal contact from unwanted sales calls, screens their e-mails, and generally ensures that they are not having their time wasted. While we know that *you* are credible, imagine how many thousands of businesses probably also want to sell products and services to your ideal buyer. If the gatekeeper let them all through, the buyer would have no time to do their 'day job'. Other companies have probably set a bad example too; they won't be as well prepared as you and they won't have put together such a quality proposition (unless, like you, they have read this book!). So the chances are, from past experience, that the gatekeeper's main response is to reject enquiries on behalf of 'the boss'. However, because you *have* done your planning and you know that you are not going to be wasting anyone's time, you can attempt to influence the gatekeeper by sharing some choice pieces of information about what you offer and the fact you're only looking for a 30-minute/1-hour exploratory chat. You can suggest that if they *don't* let you 'through the gate', and subsequently the boss does meet you, they may well be reprimanded for being so determined to keep you in abeyance, since you do have something that will genuinely be of interest etc. It might work, but if it doesn't you have to work out how to bypass them. It can be done.

There are various ways of making an initial contact, and some do go under the radar of a gatekeeper. You need to appraise the methods, what you think is most like 'your style' (what you feel is most comfortable for you) and what will be most effective. You probably will need to use a combination of two or three approaches to get the result you want. If you've ever come across NLP (neuro-linguistic programming) you may have heard about how different people are convinced differently and also how they absorb information differently. You need to convince your ideal contact to have an exploratory meeting with you. They might be 'multiple convincers' or 'time-based convincers'. Multiple convincers need to have heard about you/been approached by you several times before they'll accept a meeting. Time-based convincers need a certain amount of time, to reflect, perhaps to refer back to your contact, before they will make a decision to proceed. They may also be auditory, visual or kinaesthetic learners – in that they absorb information best by hearing, seeing or doing something – so you need to ensure that your approach includes a mix of these types of communication. You must appreciate that if you don't initially get the response you want it isn't the buyer being difficult. You need to make sure that your approach to a person you don't yet know is structured so as to account for the different styles of learning and different ways that people are convinced, so that with your approach you can confidently get through to any type of person.

So, considering the learning styles and different ways that people are convinced, Figure 8.1 reviews some of the ways in which you can make an initial contact.

FIGURE 8.1   Reviewing the different methods of making an initial contact

Method of contact	Which learning style this is effective for	Which convincer style this is effective for	My advice
Phone	As a phone call has no visual element, this will be best for anyone who is auditory. If you're dealing with a visual or kinaesthetic person you will probably feel that a phone call wasn't very successful.	As a phone call cannot be referred back to, it is less likely to have impact on time-based convincers, who like to dwell on things for a period of time and ideally refer back to something. You can somewhat cover both convincer types by agreeing to call back (or make contact via a different means, eg e-mail) in a period of time where you reiterate your points.	I would advise that a phone call follows on from a less intrusive approach such as an e-mail or letter. A phone call out of the blue can be considered to be a 'cold call' and is generally not welcomed. Some people will find a phone call ideal, but many others feel that it interrupts them, which of course it does. In my experience I would not make a first contact by phone. Instead I'd send some other form of initial communication and advise that I *will* be calling, indicating when. This is more polite than wading straight in.

FIGURE 8.1 *continued*

Method of contact	Which learning style this is effective for	Which convincer style this is effective for	My advice
E-mail	As there is no sound to an e-mail you may assume it is mainly visual. However, some auditory people 'hear' the words in their mind as they read the text, so it can be more effective than a call, which has no effect on a visual person. An e-mail can also include links to video content, which is both visual and auditory content. There is little in an e-mail to engage a kinaesthetic learner.	The e-mail can be deleted, and that's a drawback. However, for a person convinced by multiple instances of contact it can be referred back to several times, and for a time-based person it can be referred back to a few days later. It leaves a more lasting opportunity than a phone call *but* has no tone of voice and you don't get a feel for the reaction of the receiver in the same way you can with a call.	I would suggest an e-mail is a good way to make initial contact, and in an initial e-mail I would state when I will be making a follow-up phone call, eg in two days' time. This makes the call less intrusive as you have told them you will call (it is expected) and it gives you an approach that touches on those with different learning styles, helping both multiple and time-based convincers owing to repetition and time delay.
Letter	Like an e-mail, a letter is only the written word so has its limitations. It obviously can't include attachments or links.	Like an e-mail, it can be referred back to and you can follow on with a call.	In modern business e-mails are plentiful but letters are rare. You may well find that a letter has a greater impact. This would be the one real benefit of sending something in the post.

FIGURE 8.1 *continued*

Method of contact	Which learning style this is effective for	Which convincer style this is effective for	My advice
Social media	Depending on the media you use, this can touch on at least two of the learning styles. It is certainly auditory, if we assume that the message is 'heard' in the mind of the reader, and it is visual as it is presented on a screen.	Social media is more about regular, repeated communication and less about having something to refer back to. In this way it is more like a phone call than an e-mail or letter, although it does depend on the media and approach. Social media does, of course, connect your message to your online profile, thus meaning that the recipient can do a bit of digging to understand a bit more about you (which if you've worked through properly the section on Look Big will all be good!).	When you connect with someone on social media you must understand that this is a personal engagement, even if the media is quite professional (such as LinkedIn), as often the message goes to a non-business e-mail address. This will of course bypass the gatekeeper. As with any approach you need to ensure that your message is relevant and appropriate.

FIGURE 8.1   *continued*

Method of contact	Which learning style this is effective for	Which convincer style this is effective for	My advice
Trade shows, conferences and other networking events	This is a great way to meet people, in person, which engages all learning styles owing to the face-to-face and interpersonal nature of the meeting.	As a meeting is likely to be brief in such an environment, you need to ensure you agree to come back to them either by phone or by e-mail, by way of follow-up, and to progress any conversation you've had. This style of engagement only works with diligent follow-up as otherwise neither convincer type is sufficiently satisfied by what is essentially a chance meeting.	This is a more random approach – you don't know who you will meet at these events, although you should have a good idea of the type of attendee.

This is an approach that depends more on luck than judgement, unless your key contact is a speaker at an event and you absolutely know they will be there. You can't rely on this approach, so while it's great when it happens, you need to be more reliant on more structured and direct approaches. |

FIGURE 8.1   *continued*

Method of contact	Which learning style this is effective for	Which convincer style this is effective for	My advice
Requesting referrals	If someone you know, who is also known and trusted by the retail buyer, refers you then you will benefit from reflected trust. People tend only to refer people they think are credible, and if the buyer trusts your connection then by default this will give them some initial trust in you. This somewhat bypasses the issue of learning style as the introduction, via whatever means, is being done by someone they know, so they will be more open to taking in that information.	Again, as the buyer already knows and trusts the person introducing you, they don't need as much time or frequency of contact to be convinced. The introducer has already secured their trust and, as with the learning style, you essentially bypass the need to go through the convincing process in the same way you might have needed to do if it were a cold contact.	This is by far the most powerful method of making initial contact. It will certainly bypass any gatekeeper. It provides you with some reflected credibility and trust, assuming that the buyer does in fact trust the person referring you (please check this out, a referral from someone they *don't* trust is very damaging to you because the emotion that is reflected on you is then distrust!). You may feel uneasy asking for a referral, but if you don't ask you don't get. As long as the person referring you understands that you'll treat their connection with respect, and that you have a quality proposal for them, you should not be uneasy about asking for their introduction.

Once you've made the first contact, followed up, and booked the exploratory meeting, you've made positive progress in the sales process. Let's look in more detail at the exploratory meeting.

Exploratory meeting

Remember, the purpose of this meeting is to 'sell' the next step – be that a more formal presentation or to submit a proposal. An exploratory meeting is often the first opportunity you'll have to spend time, 1-2-1, with your key contact. While you obviously must focus on the outcome – agreement to move to the next step – it's critical that during this meeting you learn as much as you possibly can from them about their business, motivations, objectives, issues, worries *and* their buying process. This information will provide you with confirmation that, as a result of all your preparation, you are on the right track, potentially furnishing you with new insights and information that you can leverage throughout the next steps. As Emma Wimhurst rightly pointed out when I spoke to her, 'there is a reason you've got two ears and one mouth – you need to use them in that ratio'. That holds true for this and all future meetings!

In the exploratory meeting you need to be asking lots of questions, making copious notes, showing a really genuine interest, being personable and being knowledgeable – not too much to think about then! As we said right from the outset, first impressions count. Bearing in mind that you probably only got the meeting because you gave the right impression remotely, you have now got to live up to that expectation. If you mess up an exploratory meeting there is little or no chance of you ever being invited back to present to the wider team.

As it's so important to get this meeting right, here are a couple of top tips to consider:

1 **Check the company dress code.** Call reception and ask. If it's casual, ask how suppliers or those attending interviews tend to dress. I believe you should always dress smartly for a meeting – it helps with your mindset and confidence, projecting a strongly positive, professional first impression.

- There is one caveat to this – I recall that when I worked for SAP (the software brand), B&Q (the UK's largest DIY retail chain) was a client. They had a completely casual dress code and expressly told visitors to dress informally. Formal dress at B&Q head office was frowned upon. In a case like this, you obviously do as you are told!

2 **Check the journey to their office/meeting location.** If you can, practise it. It may sound silly but you *must* be sure that you can arrive on time, in plenty of time, unflustered. If you arrive very early you can always wait in reception or go and get a drink in a café nearby.

- Don't arrive ridiculously early; you might look a bit desperate – 10–15 minutes before you are expected is quite reasonable, up to 30 minutes if you let reception know you are early (perhaps the journey was better than expected). I would advise that you ask that the receptionist doesn't announce you have arrived until closer to the meeting time, say about 10 minutes before. Just let them know you'll sit and wait and come back to them when you'd like them to call through for you. I don't think it matters if you are announced early, but play it safe and avoid putting undue stress on the person you're waiting to meet – no one likes to feel rushed or as if they've kept someone waiting (even if their visitor was the one who was too early.)

3 **Check the agenda points.** Ideally, when you agreed the meeting you will have agreed the objective. Make sure you have a couple of clear agenda points, and include introductions so that the person you are meeting can also do some talking. As mentioned above, you want to get as much information as possible from them, so allow time for them to explain their current position relative to your proposition.

4 **Check the name of the PA/secretary.** So that when you arrive, if you are greeted by them you can say 'hello [name], good to meet you, thanks for helping organize this meeting' or similar – it's always good practice to be friendly with the gatekeeper!

5 **Check the timings**. Don't allow the meeting to overrun but be prepared for it to start late. In my experience retailers have a bad habit of being late for meetings, often held up by colleagues who allowed their previous meetings to overrun. Don't consider it to be a snub; they are busy people and as this is only an exploratory meeting you must realize that if something more urgent comes up you will be deprioritized.

6 **Check your notes and preparation**. Make sure you have a clear picture in your mind about how you will present yourself, how you'll introduce your business, and how you will give them enough information, without being overwhelming, for them to want to bring you in for a formal presentation, or to ask you to submit a proposal.

7 **Check who you are meeting**. Is this a 1-2-1 with the key contact or will others be invited in? It can be quite unsettling if you expected an informal meeting with one person, to be taken through to a room with several people around the table.

Assuming you have had a positive exploratory meeting, the buyer likes you and your proposition, you'll be moving forward in the process. Depending on the process it may be a presentation, it may be a proposal. We'll look at both in the next two sections.

The proposal

In the last chapter I outlined what is typically expected in a formal proposal – but, of course, based on the outcomes of the exploratory meeting you may well have a far clearer understanding of what the retailer specifically wants from you by way of content.

You also need to reflect on all that you have heard from them – are your assumptions valid? Was your research thorough? As a result of what you have learnt, you might need to reconsider your 'story' and the key reasons why the retailer should be buying from you.

Depending on what you now know about the process, the people involved, who wants the proposal and why, you can tailor your approach to it.

Key considerations for the submission of a proposal are:

1 Can you get the person who asked you to provide it to have a quick run through of it with you, in draft, before you finalize it? If you put this across as in their interests – 'you don't want to waste anyone's time, you just want to make sure you're on the right lines, working at the level of detail they need etc' – you may get the buyer to actually help you in writing it, in so much as they will give you feedback to help you make it better and to help them sell you/your proposition to their colleagues.

2 When do they want it by? What are their deadlines, who is it to be sent out to? What specifically is it needed for? Sometimes a proposal will contribute to a board presentation where your buyer will be angling for budget sign-off to go forward with your project. Sometimes it will feed into a range review or a review of proposed product trials. If you know when it's needed by and where it will be used, you can ensure you also highlight key, relevant points of interest.

3 How do they want it delivered? You may be asked simply to send it as an attachment to an e-mail; however, in some cases you might be asked to produce a number of spiral-bound full-colour printed copies. Make sure, if there are strict guidelines for submitting a proposal, especially if it forms part of a competitive tender, that you follow them. I've seen a team of people who were in a competitive tender for a major software project at a retailer (a project worth several million pounds) have their proposal rejected because it was not received before the deadline. It was only about 10 minutes late but the corporate procurement team refused to allow it to go forward as, clearly, if they were willing to miss a deadline at this early stage, they were not a supplier that the business would want to work with. Several days of effort wasted for being 10 minutes late. The lesson is to be cautious, don't leave anything until the last minute and double check the specific requirements, triple check in fact, to make sure you won't fall at the final hurdle.

Apart from that, there isn't much to say about the proposal. Either you will have been told when to expect them to come back to you, or, in your covering e-mail/letter, you can state when you will contact them to discuss moving forward. Chances are a good proposal will lead to a formal presentation. It might be that you are invited to present the highlights of your proposal and leave behind the full documentation for later reading. Either way, I doubt you'll sell to a retailer without at some point delivering a full and more formal presentation, so we'll look at that now.

The formal presentation

In this meeting you should be completely and utterly prepared; you have done the research, you've had conversations with the key influencer, the buyer, and you're now coming back to present a proposition so compelling, so in tune with their needs, that they'll bite your hand off. Well, that's the plan anyway.

The outcome of this meeting might be a request to submit a detailed proposal, something they can 'sign off'. Ultimately, though, you should imagine this meeting as the opportunity for you to actually sell them your full proposition and get a decision to move forward to the negotiation phase. Remember, it's during the negotiation phase (when there is already agreement in principle to purchase from you) that you agree the terms, pricing and other details necessary for the retailer to be able to sign a contract to you. As I've said before, there is no point even entering into a negotiation until such time as they've made it quite clear they intend to buy, hence why that is covered in the next chapter.

As a result of everything that's gone before – meetings, conversations etc – you should be clear as to what is expected of you in a formal presentation. You should check that what you prepared as an outline generic presentation in the preparation stage still touches on all of the most relevant points, especially now you have a better understanding of this specific retailer.

Here are some top tips to consider before your formal presentation:

1 **Check the date**, time slot and that a room has been booked for the session. If it is a long session, enquire if they expect you to

make time on the agenda for a break mid-way. See if they intend to book any refreshments for attendees in the session. Confirm the facilities in the room – what do you need to bring?

a You will typically be expected to use a presentation tool such as PowerPoint as a visual aid – you need to know if there is a laptop, projector and screen or if you should bring any of these items.

b Do you need a flipchart/whiteboard and, if so, are these in the room?

c What facilities are there for presenting the actual product? If it's a consumer product, do you need to make special arrangements to bring in samples? If it's a service, eg software or some form of business solution, can you provide a live demonstration of the solution?

   – Will you need a live internet connection and, if so, can that be provided? If not, can you run offline or bring a device to connect you to the internet?

d Do they expect you to provide a pack to review during the presentation or to provide as a leave-behind? If so, for how many people?

2 Confirm the agenda – what they expect you to cover.

   – Make sure you plan the agenda carefully, allowing the right amount of time for each key section you plan to cover as well as building in breaks and time for questions.

3 Confirm the attendees – ask for the name and job title of all those invited. Try to find out a bit about all of them; again, turning to LinkedIn may prove very handy.

   – Are they expecting to meet others from your business? If your operating model is just you at the helm with a team of outsourced support staff/consultants/suppliers called upon as and when required, do you need to organize for some of the extended team to join you in the meeting, to tackle specific questions or simply to back you up and help you in the 'looking big' department?

4 As before, check the dress code and journey times. Arrive in plenty of time to get set up.

5 Prepare for difficult questions – rehearse the presentation as I advised in Chapter 7 on preparation. Make sure that any new content you've added in light of what you've learnt since the exploratory meeting makes sense in the context of your 'standard' presentation.

- Know the details about the proposition, pricing, service promise – if necessary take a reference document with you, for your eyes only, so if quizzed on anything specific you can say 'let me just check that, I want to make sure I give you accurate information' – you can then refer to your notes. This will engender more trust than being unsure and making errors.

6 Make sure you end on a high and with time for questions. You could potentially invite anyone with questions relating specifically to their functional area to contact you directly, especially if it is a particularly technical question that may be of no interest to the rest of the audience. Make sure you are asking questions to confirm understanding, to confirm that they buy into your proposition, and that you are moving the audience towards confirming the intent to purchase from you, subject to negotiation.

7 Confirm timescales for feedback and follow up at the end of the session. Thank them for having you. Leave them with a positive impression and don't come across as desperate. No matter how friendly everyone is being, you should remain on your professional guard – don't give anything away that could pop up to your peril in a negotiation!

Assuming your presentation goes well, you'll leave feeling positive with a confirmed follow-up action to progress to the next steps. Ideally you'll receive a call from the buyer that says 'we are keen to move forward with your proposal, so we'd like to invite you in to agree terms of business' – and that's where your negotiations begin. Of course, before we dash off on to that, there is one aspect that is so integral to the sales process that you'll get nowhere without it.

I've saved the most important consideration, the process that keeps things moving in the right direction, to last. Before we move to negotiations we're going take some time to talk about following up.

Following up

In my view the key to success in the sales process depends on the quality and diligence of follow-up. If you don't keep on top of the process, and keep it moving forward, it will go 'cold'. A retail buyer has a million things to do and the most successful suppliers will be the ones who were exceptionally tenacious, keeping the focus on their follow-ups, with a planned approach, and at every stage an agreement as to when the next contact will take place.

Ideally you should keep records of where you are at with all your prospects. Customer relationship management (CRM) tools are often considered to be the solution to this; however, if you don't have an established process or an embedded set of behaviours, with the best will in the world a clever system won't help. Before investing in CRM tools I would advise that you simply keep records in a spreadsheet, something that you can sort and filter.

Thinking about the process outlined above, let's look at all the points for follow-up – you can then create a spreadsheet template to enable you to track where you are with each potential customer. This approach also means that others working with you can get a quick snapshot of where you are at and know what's required as next steps.

Example follow-up tracking

1 **During the initial contact:** you should propose some dates for an exploratory meeting. It can say: 'I've suggested some dates; if I don't hear from you before the end of this week, I'll give you a call next week to arrange a suitable time.'

   – On your tracker you need to include a note to that effect, and the due date for the planned action. You can also add this to your e-mail system; something like Outlook is a great tool. In Outlook you can set reminders on sent e-mails (to alert you to take action on the due date), create specific tasks (with due dates and reminders), or add calendar entries to do specific things at a date and time. You should use whatever works for you. Personally I find that maintaining an overview of what I need to do in a spreadsheet, backed up with flags and alerts on e-mails in Outlook, works best for me.

2 **Before the exploratory meeting**: once booked, make sure you follow up a couple of days before, to reconfirm timings and agenda points or to ask any questions.

– This is a risk; they may see this contact point as an opportunity to cancel the meeting. I have a great friend who is a highly regarded sales coach who would strongly advise *not* to do this. We've debated the point and agreed to disagree. Having worked in big retail companies I know what it's like; things come up and meetings get cancelled. I think confirming is a must. If your meeting gets cancelled more than once you may realize they are 'fobbing you off'. If they genuinely are struggling to fit in the meeting with you, your flexibility and willingness to rebook will do no harm, in fact it may well endear you to the buyer all the more. I do think it's better to reconfirm everything, to manage their expectations and plan the meeting, even if that means you end up rebooking it. To turn up and discover that the buyer is not prepared for you or has been dragged away to deal with an emergency would be worse, especially if you'd paid a lot for your travel or wasted a lot of your time.

3 **After the exploratory meeting**: after this meeting you need to follow up to finalize the details of the agreed next steps. I find that a simple 'thank you' e-mail, replaying the key points of the meeting, is a good way to do this.

– If you don't get confirmation of next steps I'd use a mixture of phone calls (and do leave a message if you get through to voice-mail) and e-mails until you get a response. No reply does not mean disinterest, it just means that they are busy. Keep trying. I've told clients before that until the retailer actually tells you that they don't want to hear from you again there is no reason why you can't contact them once or twice a week until you get what you want. Of course, if they *do* tell you to stop contacting them, you have to respect that. More often, however, they'll say 'we're simply not in a position to look at this for the next six months' – to which, of course, you respond – 'that's great – I'll drop you a line then'. And you make a note to do so.

4 **Before the proposal is sent**: as touched on before, if you have been invited to send a proposal I would always attempt to get some feedback from your contact, to ensure you're heading in the right direction with the content you've prepared. It may not be something they can do or have time for, but you should try. If not, you simply need to double check the details with them regarding submission requirements and confirm what the timelines are thereafter. If they say 'we'll come back to you within two weeks of submitting the proposal', you can answer 'great, in which case if I've not heard from you by then I'll drop you a line/give you a call'.

5 **After the proposal is sent**: as above – chase them up for a response if they haven't come back to you by the time they said they would. You can also give them a call to confirm receipt if you feel that is important.

   – When you hear from them you should be pressing for the next contact point, which may be to book a date for the formal presentation. At that stage, and in line with their timescales, you could suggest a few slots that would be suitable for you so that they are focused on booking something with you.

6 **Before the formal presentation**: also as outlined above, contact them to check all the details and to confirm what's expected.

7 **After the formal presentation**: on the day, at the end of the presentation, confirm with your key contact how you'll follow up together – then immediately reconfirm that with an e-mail. Make sure you let them know when you'll call back if you've not heard from them. The focus at this stage is on the meeting

to move forward, to confirm their intent to purchase from you and to arrange a time to scope out the rules of engagement/ terms of business (which essentially is your negotiation point).

As you can see, by doing this you are keeping the process moving forward, you are in the driving seat, and you are always managing expectations and setting dates/deadlines for the next action. Where you do leave the ball in their court, you tell them that should you not hear from them you will pick it up and proactively contact them. This kind of rigour will ensure that there is no ambiguity, and it will establish you as a professional who is structured, organized, eager to progress and respectful of the time of others. It's a good way to start a relationship as they will understand that should they come to work with you, when you say you will do something, you absolutely will do it.

Some people are fearful of follow-up – it can also be tedious – but diligently following up proves you are a serious business person, determined and focused. And it gets results. A diligent supplier is the kind of supplier we all want, so while you may think you are nagging or chasing, in fact you are building up their trust in your ability to keep your promises. If you keep that in mind when following up, you should feel a great deal more comfortable about what is a necessary, critical process.

Wrapping up

In this chapter we have focused on the sales process, covering how to:

- plan the sales process;
- approach each step of the process;
- follow up.

So, assuming you've followed up diligently and you have been successful in the sales process, you will now have had confirmation from the retailer that they want to buy your product or services. You will have been invited into a negotiation. In the final chapter of this part on Pitch Big we're going to explore that further.

09

Negotiation

Introduction

In this chapter we will consider some of the discussion points that could come up in the negotiation stage, and how you can tackle them. I can't restate often enough how you should *not* even be considering a negotiation until you have some indication from the retailer that they intend to proceed to contract with you, subject to a successful negotiation.

In this chapter we will discuss:

- what a negotiation is and when it should take place;
- negotiation options – what approaches there are to give both sides an outcome that they want without either side feeling they have conceded too much;
- why, in some instances, it is better for your business to walk away from what appears to be a 'great opportunity'.

The ideal outcome of any successful negotiation is that both parties can confidently proceed with what will be a mutually beneficial working relationship for the long term.

What is a negotiation and when should it happen?

The dictionary defines a negotiation as a mutual discussion and arrangement of the terms of a transaction or agreement. It sounds so simple, yet most of the business owners I meet are nervous of negotiations; some are more than nervous, they're actually scared of this process.

I think this fear of negotiation stems from the horror stories people tell about when a negotiation has turned sour or when one party dominated. Certainly, if previous negotiations have not been focused on a mutually beneficial discussion, where one side has demanded compliance with their terms, not allowing any concession when the other party attempts to offer a trade-off, it won't have been a good experience. This 'my way or the highway' approach is sadly how many retailers have behaved towards suppliers in the past. It's therefore not that surprising that some people have had bad experiences, and I am also not surprised when clients who want to become suppliers to retailers are dreading what to expect when it is time for them to enter into a negotiation. Luckily, things have changed and retail buyers are not the ogres they were once painted to be. In the main, should you reach the negotiation stage, you will find that the retailer is keen to find a mutually beneficial way forward – they'll have already invested a lot of time in getting to know you, so it's in their interest not to let the process fall over at the final hurdle.

Of course, if you are fearful of a face-to-face negotiation you should seek some specific training to hone your skills and give you greater confidence in your abilities. I am not going to cover that here; this chapter focuses on what you can practically do to prepare for a negotiation. The purpose is to guide you as to what reasonable trade-offs you might consider offering when pressed to concede on specific points.

As mentioned above, even the largest retailers usually aim to enter a negotiation to achieve an optimal outcome for both parties; the old, adversarial retailer–supplier relationships are becoming a thing of the past. Retailers recognize that treating suppliers fairly is better for their suppliers and for their reputations. While there is usually no doubt that the balance of power, in terms of sheer size of business and financial strength, is weighted in favour of the retailer, this is less often 'used' by the retailer to get the supplier to bend to what they want.

As I explained in the previous chapter, a negotiation should *only* happen once you have confirmed that the buyer wants to buy and that the seller wants to sell. The negotiation can't take place prior as, in line with its definition, it's about arranging the terms of a transaction or agreement. These arrangements can only be discussed when you know that both parties will move forward to a contractual relationship based on the outcome of that negotiation. For instance, how can you negotiate a price or volume-related discount unless you know that the retailer plans to buy X quantity in a given period of time? How can you agree the logistics service levels, packaging requirements and delivery schedule until you know how many items the retailer needs, delivered where, for when? It is possible that in the sales process you could be asked something like 'do you offer volume-related discounts?' and of course you can answer, 'if you are planning to stock our product then this would certainly be something we'd review with you in more detail at the negotiation stage', or you can head off those sorts of question in the sales process with reference to a standard price list, which might be structured to allow price-breaks subject to higher order quantities.

Essentially the outcome of the negotiation should be that both parties have taken the time to listen to, and understand, the drivers behind the needs and wants of the other. Sometimes what seem to be ridiculous requests are of paramount importance. Let me share a case study that really brings this to life.

CASE STUDY

An example of why both parties should understand the drivers behind specific requests was when a retailer had specified that a supplier ensure the location of the label on the delivery packaging be in a very precise position. It was critical to the retailer, but the supplier didn't understand why, thinking they were just being picky or difficult. However, when the supplier presented deliveries that were not precisely labelled, these were returned to the supplier, along with a hefty charge based on the retailer's handling fee due to the supplier presenting a non-compliant delivery. When this happened to the supplier they thought that this was incredibly petty and got very frustrated about it. The goods had been returned, so they'd get no payment until they were re-presented correctly *and* they now had a failed delivery charge to pay as well! The supplier was planning to call the buyer to complain about this ridiculous situation. Luckily, before they made the call they read through the detailed terms of business, to identify what the specific terms were with regard to passing on handling charges relating to failed deliveries. At this point the supplier discovered that they'd avoided an embarrassing, potentially damaging, phone call. It was clearly stated in the terms regarding deliveries that due to the retailer's fully automated warehousing system deliveries could not be accepted that did not have the labels correctly positioned for the robotic scanners to book-in. Instead, these boxes would fail the booking-in process and due to the manual intervention required to handle failed boxes, for each box that the system failed there would be a fee passed on to the supplier whose items had breached the delivery specification. It was all there, on the terms. So the supplier called the retailer, not to complain, but to apologize for the recent batch of poorly labelled boxes and to promise a 100 per cent compliant shipment next time.

In this example the supplier should have checked each of the terms carefully, to ensure that they knew exactly what they were getting into. At the negotiation stage, they should have raised their concerns about any terms that were unexpected or likely to incur them costs/ difficulties. In their excitement to secure a great new retail client they eagerly signed the contract without the requisite consideration for the consequences. A requirement that seemed petty at first, once understood by the supplier, seemed entirely reasonable. Another key point about a negotiation is to take the time to really understand the reasons why you are being asked to conform to the retailer's terms of business, as then you'll be better informed as to what you can challenge and what aspects are unlikely to be open for discussion. In the example above, there would have been no flexibility on the label position, but then had the supplier read the details and understood why that was the case, they would have been unlikely to request flexibility on that point anyway.

In any negotiation each of the parties should acknowledge the requirements of the other and commit to return with a proposal as to how they can accommodate the requirements. The most important thing to remember in a negotiation is that if something is not an issue to you, you can give it to your future customer easily and at no cost. If it is important to them then you have the opportunity to trade. Negotiations are all about trades and equality. When you give, you should also receive something in respect of that. What may be easy for you to give could be of huge importance to the retailer, and similarly something of great value or benefit to you could be very easily given by them. If you make a point of always requesting something in return for anything that you give, both parties can come away with a positive outcome, having achieved most of what they wanted from the deal. This is often referred to as a 'win–win' situation.

Points to negotiate to get your desired outcome

When it comes to negotiating, it's important to have a clear plan of what you want to achieve from the discussions. This should include:

- A detailed list of your ideal outcomes, in priority order.
- A list of what you anticipate them asking of you.
- A list of any 'extras' you'd like to have or variations to standard terms that you would want. Should you be pressed on a point, these are the things that you can ask for, by way of a trade, should you concede.
    - Where relevant, try to match these to the list of things the retailer is likely to negotiate on, so that should you be asked to concede on X, you only agree if they can offer you Y.

Make sure you prioritize your ideal outcomes; this is key to ensuring you get a win–win. If these factors are too important to concede on or to give up, you will know when you need to consider walking away (which we discuss at the end of this chapter). As each business owner is likely to have different desired outcomes, or different prioritization of their outcomes, I won't attempt to second-guess that with examples. Do take the time though to make a list and think about what matters to you.

Figure 9.1 is a table of possible negotiation points that the retailer might want to discuss with you; it's not exhaustive, but should give you an idea of what to expect. I've also included a couple of ways you might want to counter some of these points.

FIGURE 9.1 Negotiation points that may be requested and how to counter them

Negotiation point	Why the retailer might ask for this	How you might be able to counter this – things you might ask for in return
Cost price	With product the simplest way to increase the retail margin is to reduce the supplier's cost price. With services the retailer will want to get the maximum input for the minimum budget.	Base any discounts on volume, so they commit to a larger order quantity. If you are a services supplier, explain that you can't offer discounts as it would compromise the quality of delivery, but propose something else you can do that may benefit them instead.
Listing fee	Applicable only to products; occasionally retailers want a one-off contribution for every store where they stock the product. It's a direct benefit to their margin before the product even begins to sell, it shows supplier commitment to the product success and it covers some of the operational costs of re-merchandising.	Obviously you can request a reduction in the listing fee to avoid the cash-flow impact. Otherwise you can offer it as a later discount off product, once you've generated margin from the retailer. Rarely will this be avoidable and actually you should already be aware of this from the pre-sales conversations with the retailer and your research of how they operate.
Exclusivity	If you have a desirable product and the retailer wants first-to-market advantage, they may want a period of exclusivity. If you have a service proposition that can help them achieve competitive advantage or that gives you access to their key business data, they may want to exclude you from working with their competitors.	Product exclusivity is a double-edged sword. It's great to be 'wanted' but not to the detriment of future sales opportunities. Ensure that any exclusive period is time limited, ideally doesn't prohibit you from selling via your own e-commerce (if you wish), and is both location (eg UK only) and retailer (eg named exclusions) specific. Try to link the period of exclusivity to a minimum initial order quantity. With services, particularly if you help them achieve competitive advantage or deal with sensitive information, you may need to agree a similar set of exclusions as with product, eg exclude only named competitors, minimum contract term and value, and obviously offer the retailer protection through strict non-disclosure agreements.

FIGURE 9.1 *continued*

Negotiation point	Why the retailer might ask for this	How you might be able to counter this – things you might ask for in return
Minimum order quantity	With product specifically you may want the retailer to buy a larger batch than they initially want. They may wish to moderate the risk of investment of stock by asking for smaller order quantities from you. This makes managing the administrative processes, and the flow of goods, onerous for all concerned.	Counterbalance the request for small minimums with a conversation about the cost of *their* management overhead for going down this route. This will include resources to raise orders, to book to stock into their systems, to match invoices etc. Try to find an optimal order size for both parties. You could potentially offer sale or return on a proportion of the stock if unsold within a given period. Leverage exclusive deals and cost price discounts to secure a respectable order quantity.
Payment terms (eg 90 days from receipt of goods for product or 90 days from invoice for services)	Obviously, if a retailer can sell the majority of stock before having to pay for it, they have the cash-flow benefit. Of course, the cost of financing the stock is covered somewhere in the supply chain. When services are delivered there is often a considerable lead time before payment is made, in part because that's the way it has always been, in part so that the retailer can begin to benefit from the service having been provided before the payment is made.	Obviously payment terms can make a huge difference to your cash flow. With product, since you are bearing the cost of financing the period between when you laid out for raw materials and when they pay for their finished product, you have to increase your margin to absorb that. If you point this out to the retailer, you could get paid more quickly, especially if you can offer credits or discounts for more rapid payment. When it comes to services it's tough, however, and in my own experience, if you simply agree the terms – 'that's fine, you can pay my invoice in 90 days and when I receive the funds I can deliver the services' – that somewhat turns things back in your favour. It won't work every time but I can assure you that it's worked for me and I'm not talking about a small retail chain, I'm talking about a couple of global mega-brands. If they want what you offer they won't want to wait, the terms are usually set by Finance and going outside of those terms can be a bit of a nuisance, but certainly not insurmountable.

FIGURE 9.1   *continued*

Negotiation point	Why the retailer might ask for this	How you might be able to counter this – things you might ask for in return
Sale or return	With product suppliers who are new to the retailer this can be a favourable approach as they are giving the product a chance to prove itself before making any major investment in stock.	Actually, for a product that is new to market this isn't a bad offer – you will be able to get your product in front of consumers. Make sure that your exposure is minimized by having only a small amount of stock issued on a sale or return basis. Make sure that the retailer knows the most effective way to merchandise the item to give it the best opportunity of selling.
Support services	With more complex and technical products, and especially with services, retailers will want the supplier to be able to provide a level of support to them in order that they have an escalation process and a point of call to resolve any issues.	Again, you should be offering some form of support to your retail clients as a matter of good business practice. If they are asking for 24/7 support and you currently only cover office hours, you need to determine the costs of extended support services and therefore what size of contract (minimum order or term of engagement) you need from the retailer to be able to put in place what they need. Of course, if you point out that you already have support, and what's included, they may decide that's enough. If you make extending your services subject to them extending their contact terms, you should also reach a win–win position.

Well, that's all great for your retail buyer but there are some negotiation points *you* might want to put to a retailer that aren't to directly counter a point they have raised. Figure 9.2 is a list of some ideas, as a starting point. You can add to this list, or create your own, being as creative as you like because all that really matters is that as a result of the negotiation you have a win–win, with a retailer client who is happy with the outcome, and a good deal for your business too.

FIGURE 9.2   Negotiation points that you may want to raise and why

Negotiation point you might want to raise	Why you might ask for this
Foot in the door opportunities – trial/proof of concept, sale or return, online only	Obviously if you can get the retailer to test your concept, be it product or service, then they're going to appreciate its potential far better.
	From running a trial in-store, to offering sale or return or even an online-only listing, anything to get your product in front of their customer may well be worth pushing for in order for you each to determine the future opportunities most effectively.
	With services, offering a sample, a trial, a free example or a proof of concept can help them, if they leveraged your proposition in a full roll-out, to see what the business benefit could be.
Provision of a full case study – why the retailer chose to work with you	Whether a product or services supplier, you ideally want to gather as many positive case studies, testimonials and endorsements as you can. These can form part of your marketing materials, helping you to attract new customers. They can also be part of your sales presentations, helping you to convince other retailers about the quality of your proposition.
	Try to get agreement that subject to meeting defined success criteria the retailer will provide a full written case study, with quotes, that you can use extensively for your PR and marketing.

FIGURE 9.2 *continued*

Negotiation point you might want to raise	Why you might ask for this
Nominated contact at the retailer to act as a customer reference, willing to take calls from potential customers	Linked to the case study point, if you have agreed with a customer that they will act as a point of contact to which you can direct potentially interested parties, this is hugely valuable. If the retailer agrees to answer questions about your service delivery as their supplier (via phone or e-mail) and act as a reference customer for you, this will go a long way to helping you secure new customers.
Joint PR – distribution of a press release by the retailer about their engagement of your services or listing of your product	Leveraging the content of your case study: if you can get the retailer to agree to issue a press release stating that they have engaged your services or listed your product, the benefit can be considerable.
	If service suppliers get this kind of coverage in key trade press it will certainly help boost profile and may lead to enquiries from interested retailers.
	Press releasing about your product to the consumer press can help to increase sales.
If you are a product supplier, request specific product placement in-store, or in the retailer's advertising etc	If you have a view as to how your product should be most effectively merchandised, you can influence this by requesting specific placement in-store. You could also ask that it is featured in any consumer-facing advertising in order to encourage sales.

FIGURE 9.2   *continued*

Negotiation point you might want to raise	Why you might ask for this
If you are a services supplier, the retailer could support you at conferences or exhibitions	Conferences, exhibitions and other events of that sort (breakfast briefings, roundtable discussions etc) are a great way to get your message across to retailers who are specifically researching services. Often you will be required to sponsor such an event to get exposure, but if you have a strong retailer case study and have negotiated that the retailer will put forward a speaker to support you at an event, then an event could be a very good investment of marketing spend. At least if you have secured agreement for such events at the point of negotiation you have the choice, should the opportunity arise.

Some of the points from this list can contribute towards the next chapter on expansion, because where your negotiations lead to a retailer agreeing to give you written case studies, for example, you can use these in your marketing and PR. In the next chapter I will be explaining how to leverage such things as case studies to enable you to increase your customer numbers and accelerate your growth. With that in mind, make sure that you do not miss the opportunity to get something agreed in a negotiation that could subsequently help you to grow your business or attract more customers. After you've read the next chapter, make sure you return to your ideas about negotiation points and add any ideas that you hadn't already thought of which will specifically help you to increase your customer base and achieve your expansion plans.

Remember that a negotiation *should* create a win–win situation, an outcome that both parties are happy to proceed with, and a viable, commercial, sustainable relationship.

Sometimes in the negotiation it becomes clear that expectations formed in the pre-sales and sales process simply can't be met. Occasionally it is necessary to walk away from a negotiation and *not* secure the retailer as your customer. This can sometimes be favourable to continuing a discussion that evidently won't meet enough of your business objectives to make it a viable or appropriate decision for you to move forward. In the final part of this chapter we'll explore that a little further.

Walking away

Sometimes negotiations expose aspects of the retailer's detailed terms of business that are so unfavourable to you/your business that it is necessary to walk away. This is still a positive outcome as you've avoided going into an agreement that is not in the best interests of your organization. It takes enormous courage to walk away from a deal, especially if it's for a sizeable order or with a well-known retailer, but you will look back on it in relief if the terms would have paralyzed your business or put you into cash-flow difficulties.

You need to clearly plan out what your no-go areas are. It will be different for every business owner, so you need to work out where your no-go position is. You might have a different perspective for each and every retailer you speak to – for example, if this is your tenth-priority target you might walk away over something that you'd concede for your first-priority target. Only you will know when the retailer has overstepped that no-go position in terms of what they are asking for. My advice is to let the retailer know immediately that this is something you simply can't concede on, and that if they are insistent on the point you would not be able to agree terms. Always try to find positive alternatives that you can offer them, other concessions you can make that might be similar to those they are proposing but less impactful on your business.

If you've done a great job of selling your proposition to the retailer it is very unlikely that you'll ever be faced with this situation, so we won't labour the point. All you need to do is make sure that you are clear and certain of your 'walk-away' points so that should the retailer refuse to move on their position you *do* walk away. The worst possible thing you could do is 'threaten' a retailer with 'if you don't drop that point of negotiation we will be unable to agree terms and will walk away from the deal proposed' and in fact still be willing to negotiate. You'll undermine your professional credibility and integrity in the eyes of the retailer and chances are they will then want to walk away in any case. The simple rule is never to make a threat that you aren't willing to follow through on.

Wrapping up

In this chapter we have explored the negotiation process, covering:

- when to negotiate;
- what points you'll consider in a negotiation;
- when it might be better for you to walk away from a 'deal'.

This process is done in order to achieve a win–win situation for both parties.

Part Three: Pitch Big – summing up

In this part we have been focusing on how to pitch your product or service to a retail buyer and achieve a successful sale.

Having completed these three chapters you will now have a far clearer view of the end-to-end sales process, including the pre-sales preparation, the selling itself, from the initial contact with the buyer through to the confirmation of intent to buy, and the pre-contract negotiations.

We have determined:

1 who your key retailer targets are and what's important to each of them;

2 what your ideal sales process involves and how you will keep it moving forward;

3 how to negotiate to achieve an optimal outcome and a long-term retailer–supplier relationship.

We're going to wrap up this part on Pitch Big with a simple checklist (Figure 9.3) for you to go through to make sure that you're clear about what the ingredients are to achieve a successful sale.

This checklist is also available for download, if you prefer, via **www.retailchampion.co.uk/selling-to-retailers/resources**.

continued on page 188

FIGURE 9.3 Part Three checklist

Area	Ingredient	Complete? (yes/no)	Action to address (if any)	Cost implications?	Priority (H/M/L)	Target date to complete
Preparation	Defining your top 10 target retail customers and ranking them in order of priority					
Preparation	Researching each retailer in detail and determining how each retailer specifically needs or benefits from your product or service					
Preparation	Creating a comprehensive proposal document that can be tailored to each retailer's requirements in the selling stage					
Preparation	Developing an outline presentation that can be tailored to each retailer's requirements in the selling stage					

Selling	Defining your ideal sales process and determining how you will approach each step			
Selling	Creating a method of tracking the sales process, recording contact with the retailer, progress made, and highlighting agreed/planned follow-up actions			
Negotiation	Planning the negotiation and prioritizing your ideal outcomes			
Negotiation	Defining your counter-requests to the most likely retailer negotiation points			
Negotiation	Developing a list of extras you might want to ask for that aren't directly related to the commercials of the sale but contribute to your wider business growth strategy			
Negotiation	Determining your 'walk-away' position			

Part Three: Pitch Big – summing up   *continued*

As always, having gone through the checklist, the onus is on you to actually implement the actions that you have identified. Having now successfully completed Part Three we're ready to move on to the last part, Part Four: Get Big, Stay Big! This section will include three chapters: Expansion, Replication and Paranoia! In the previous three parts you have done all the hard work, so this is where you start to use everything you've developed to grow the business. You're on the home-straight!

PART FOUR
Get Big, Stay Big!

In Part Three we focused on the pitch: the pre-sales preparation, selling and negotiation. The result of a successful sale is the beginning of your business growth, so this part is all about how to get big by achieving more successful sales – and how to stay big by taking your business to the next level and making sure you keep it there!

This part, the final part of the process, is all about creating a growth wave and then ensuring that your business is able to keep the momentum going. It includes three chapters: Expansion, Replication and Paranoia!

- Expansion is all about creating an upward spiral of growth. By delivering on your customer promises you can secure their loyalty and trust. Having proven your business to your initial customers, expansion is about leveraging case studies and success stories in order to attract the interest of new customers through PR, marketing and events.

- Replication is about the mechanics of sustainable growth. Building on what we discussed in Chapter 6 on scalability, we will ensure that you embed a robust, repeatable business model. We'll focus on the importance of having an effective back office in addition to the core operational functions. We'll wrap up by reflecting on your role as the owner of a growing enterprise.

- Paranoia! is the final chapter. It's easy to get comfortable and enjoy success. My advice, if you want not only to get big but to stay big, is to be just as hungry for success as you ever were. There will be plenty of new start-ups, who will be as driven and ambitious as you were at the beginning, snapping at your heels, trying to take some of your hard-earned market share. The only thing that will ensure complacency doesn't set in is a healthy dose of paranoia!

At the end we'll recap on the key components of how to 'get big, stay big', with a checklist for you to go through to make sure you've got all the necessary ingredients in place.

Expansion

10

Introduction

In this chapter we focus on how you can leverage all the hard work done to sell to a retailer in order to attract more customers and expand your business.

We will:

- discuss the importance of delivering on your promises to ensure your customers are more than happy to support you and your business;
- consider how to leverage your customer case studies to develop an effective PR and marketing campaign, reviewing a whole range of possible options;
- reflect on how expansion is far simpler if you can create an upward spiral of growth.

Of course, how that growth is achieved will be what we look at in Chapter 11 on replication.

Delivering on your promises to secure customer loyalty

If you can develop strong relationships with your customers such that you can be trusted to deliver time and time again, you are likely to secure their long-term loyalty.

Remember what I said right back in Chapter 1, when we talked about positioning?

When your brand makes promises, implied or explicit, these set expectations with your customer.

If you fail to deliver on those promises you will fail to deliver the expected customer experience.

You *must* deliver on the expectations you've set from all your interactions with that client, and when you do, consistently, you'll also be able to approach them and ask them to provide a case study or contribute to a success story which can then be used to help attract new customers.

Loyalty is also important for another reason. There are really only two ways that your business can expand:

1 increasing your turnover with your existing customers;

2 increasing the number of customers you have (and retaining those you have already).

In the beginning it is far easier for you to expand your level of business with customers who already know and trust you. The key is that once you've sold to them, as long as you deliver on your promises, it's far easier to retain them than to start from scratch with a customer who's essentially a stranger to you.

Grant Leboff, a friend of mine, talks about this concept in his book *Sticky Marketing*. He describes an upside-down funnel, something like Figure 10.1.

FIGURE 10.1   Upside-down funnel analogy for growing your customer base through retention

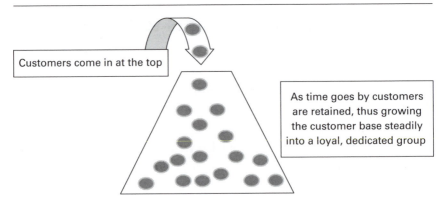

Of course, it's not only about retaining customers; as I touched on earlier, you can leverage the positive experience your existing customers have had with you to form part of your marketing strategy, attracting new customers to you owing to the positive PR and rave reviews that they see about you from your existing customer base.

It can be something that you can include in a negotiation, as mentioned in the previous chapter. From the outset you can include terms that state that, subject to your business meeting defined success criteria, the customer will support your business development activities by providing PR about your appointment as a supplier, or a case study/testimonial/success story. However, that alone will make little difference to you – it's how you leverage the content that counts.

Using case studies to attract more interest from potential customers

Assuming you've agreed with your customers that you've done a fantastic job, exactly as you promised, you'll now have some great collateral that you need to make best use of. Essentially, what you need to do now is leverage your compelling customer case studies to create PR and marketing materials that will attract interested parties to contact you for more details – I call this 'attraction marketing'.

This works, and I want to share a case study to bring this to life. Again, I can't give away the name of the company in question but at least it should demonstrate just how retailers do love to buy from brands which are tried, tested and trusted by other retailers.

CASE STUDY

In 2009 a niche marketing company, with just two members of staff at the time, managed to secure a trial of a new approach they had developed with the UK's largest retailer – Tesco. It was very successful and the marketing manager agreed to allow the results of the trial to be referenced in sales presentations to any other non-supermarket retailers.

Thanks to being able to use the initial trial results from Tesco, this tiny and relatively unknown business was able to get a foot in the door at other retailers. Within six months they managed to secure three more trials – Crabtree & Evelyn (luxury toiletries), Coast (fashion) and T.M.Lewin (tailoring). It was unlikely that these retailers would have been willing to speak to the niche provider if they had not been able to talk about their Tesco case study.

These three trials were also successful. On this occasion the retailers agreed to allow their results to be used as case study examples in a presentation delivered at a conference as well as in e-mail marketing.

Thanks to these case studies, the company was able to secure two further significant retail and hospitality clients, which enabled them to grow their team to a total of five within the year. They continue to go from strength to strength.

This example proves that leveraging past client success stories is a really effective way to attract new customers. Although the example above didn't involve a full-blown written case study, the fact that they were allowed to make reference to well-respected retailers, and demonstrate how they had added value, carried considerable weight. However, if you want to prepare a comprehensive case study, it should include some key elements:

- Why the retailer selected you.
  - What gap/issue your proposition filled/fixed.
  - The attributes that attracted them to you.
- How it has been successful for the retailer.
  - The benefits that the retailer has realized since working with you.
  - Whether this matched/exceeded their expectations.
- Whether the retailer would recommend you to others.
  - A glowing testimonial...

The basic content of your case study can be leveraged in a variety of ways; I've listed some of the most likely/popular in Figure 10.2 and appraised them according to the pros/cons. Obviously you'd choose the ones most relevant to your business and most suitable for the engagement of your ideal customer. It would make sense to use a mix of methods for maximum effect.

FIGURE 10.2 The pros and cons of various PR and marketing methods that leverage your client case studies

Marketing method	Pros	Cons
Press release: You can take key extracts from the case study, including key quotes from the client and any facts and figures that they are happy to allow into the public domain, and issue that to press contacts. This is considerably more effective, in terms of positioning your business as a great company to approach, if the release is worded so as to appear to come from your client (who is also likely to be the more well-known brand).	Excellent route to target the press that your ideal customers read. May lead to press interviewing you/your customer for more details so you can get potentially a better feature.	You may need to engage a PR agency who can help you put the release together and more importantly distribute it to the key press you want to reach – there will be a cost to this, but it is likely to reap rewards as you'll get better coverage and considerably better return on investment for PR services than if, for example, you paid for advertising.
Your website: You should make good use of any positive customer comment on your website. I'd suggest using key quotes on the home page in a highly visible location, having links to case studies/your clients, and having a news page where you can feature press releases. This ensures maximum visibility of the content most likely to attract the interest of potential new customers.	As this is your own website you can determine where the content works best. As long as the content is approved by your client you won't have to seek sign-off in order to make the content live.	Depending on who supplies your website services there may be some cost incurred to add this content, but again this should be entirely reasonable given the credibility it will add to have the content on your site.

FIGURE 10.2   *continued*

Marketing method	Pros	Cons
Blog/social media: You can reference the approved case study content in any blog you publish or on any of your social media content. In addition, you can ask for a LinkedIn endorsement about you from your key contact at your client. If you can get a video testimonial you can add this to YouTube and this can be very powerful both on your YouTube channel and embedded in your website and blog.	Social media can help drive traffic back to your main website, which hopefully will include the call to action that compels the interested party to contact you. It is free.	Social media will add credibility to your claims but it should be part of the whole 'attraction marketing' process and not the only thing you do. You can't be targeted with most social media, as it's more random than focused.
Brochure/flyers: It's important to have some form of physical material – it helps with those who are kinaesthetic learners (something physical to hold) and for those who like to reflect on something over a period of time or reflect frequently before they will make a decision. You can use snippets of key quotes, whole paragraphs of text, or even get the whole case study designed into a nice document that you can leave with a potential client.	Very useful as a reference document. Brings the brand and the case study to life.	Some cost for design/production. You need to ensure the materials are a quality that fits your positioning – think presentation!

FIGURE 10.2   *continued*

Marketing method	Pros	Cons
Exhibition stand: You can use key customer quotes, attributed to the customer, to attract attention to the graphics used on your stand.	Similar to a brochure/flyer, it brings the brand to life. Using snippets of testimonials/customer endorsements (attributed to those customers and possibly also with their brand logos if they are well known) can capture the interest of a passer-by, perhaps making them decide to stop and ask for more information. This is less direct but certainly an effective way of getting attention at a crowded event/show.	Not only are there costs associated with design/ production, but having space at an exhibition/ show is often a considerable investment. While your case study may attract passing visitors, you must be sure that you will attract your ideal customers and not just people who are interested but unlikely ever to buy from you.
Speaking events: Conferences and exhibitions as well as other similar events often invite guest speakers to share their success stories with the audience. Some of these pay speakers, others expect speakers to contribute for free, and many expect those who can benefit commercially from speaking at the conference to pay for the opportunity.	There is probably no better way to get your message across, and earn the trust of an audience, than by sharing your case study. This is even more powerful if you have a representative from your retail client with you, either backing you up or participating in the talk. If you can share your success story in a frank, open and honest way, you don't need to sell. This approach invites the interested parties in the audience to connect with you when the time is right for them. This kind of approach may not yield immediate results, but it enables you/the business to increase profile, and links back to what we discussed in Chapter 2 on presence, about being seen as the go-to brand for what you offer.	Some people find speaking in public daunting, and this may apply to you or indeed to your client. Often businesses are expected to pay for the privilege of addressing an audience, as event organizers know that this is a good way for you to drum up interest in your brand/offering. Your customer may not be permitted to speak alongside you owing to corporate communications policies and other restrictions on them – you have to remember they are probably an employee, answerable to a large organization, and don't have the flexibility you have when it comes to how they spend their time and what activities they get involved in.

FIGURE 10.2   *continued*

Marketing method	Pros	Cons
E-mail marketing: If you have a mailing list that you regularly send newsletters or other content to, then it goes without saying that if you have a news feature about a particular client case study, you can highlight this in your regular e-mail and include a link for the reader to click through to read full details (usually on your website).	This is a very direct approach. It often works best to give a brief introduction to the case study as part of the news feature and to include a link to the full case study on your website. You can draw attention to your case study this way and increase traffic to your website. The reader may then take an interest, browsing around the site. Subject to your content being well written and well presented, they should learn sufficient about you to want to make contact with you when the time is right.	This really only works when you have an e-mail list that you can send out to. These can be purchased, but of course that carries a cost. You have to avoid overmarketing by e-mail as you will risk unsubscribes (reducing the number of names on your database), or worse, being reported for spamming!
Direct mail: Similar to e-mail marketing, only using physical post. If you can create a quality letter and include your case study/brochure/flyer with that, sending it directly to all of your target retailers (those who are most likely to identify with the content of the case study), then this can be very effective. This is a good way to approach the initial contact stage as discussed in Chapter 8 on selling.	Often this can be considered less intrusive than e-mail, and, given that most communications these days are electronic, this can also be a unique, more personal, approach. It can also be part of a more tailored, targeted 'initial contact' approach, leveraging the case study to make it an even more compelling reason to meet.	Can be costly as it requires printed media, the list to distribute to, and postage.

FIGURE 10.2 *continued*

Marketing method	Pros	Cons
Tele-marketing: Again, like direct mail, this is more targeted, less of the 'attraction marketing' approach and more of the initial contact approach in your selling cycle. The reason it features here is that you will be referencing the case study in your call, inviting an exploratory meeting to take them through the case study, and suggesting that you'd like to explore how they could also benefit from a similar approach.	When this works, it is direct and targeted; however, like the e-mail and direct mail approaches, this is more of a lead-generation exercise than true attraction marketing.	Costs include the data, the resources to make the calls, and the call charges. It can be considered quite intrusive – some people react badly to any form of tele-marketing, so you need to have a skilled tele-marketer to undertake the process, who is able to stick to the topic and deal with any hostility.
Referral marketing: This is unlike any other form of marketing. We touched upon referrals as a way to make initial contact in Chapter 8. If those who were willing to refer you can now use your case study materials to better get across what you offer and the value you add to the retailer, it will enable them to give you more, better-quality referrals which may well lead to more exploratory meetings.	As touched on in Chapter 8, using referrals is a great way to create interest in you and in your brand via a trusted third party. If you can provide the key messages from your case study to those willing to refer you, it will not only give them greater confidence in making the referral for you but also provide them with the key points to share with the person they are referring you to. Like the previous few approaches, this is a combination of attraction marketing and generating an initial interest.	There are few drawbacks to this strategy other than that it is a 1-2-1 approach and therefore not something that can be scaled up by allocating more resources to it.

Creating an upward spiral of growth

However you go about it, using your happy customers to form part of the process of attracting new customers will be very effective. Often I speak at events and to clients about creating an upward spiral of growth – visually I use something a bit like Figure 10.3, which, like Grant's 'upside-down funnel', represents my concept of attraction marketing really well.

FIGURE 10.3   The four-part upward cycle of growth: attraction, conversion, retention and referral

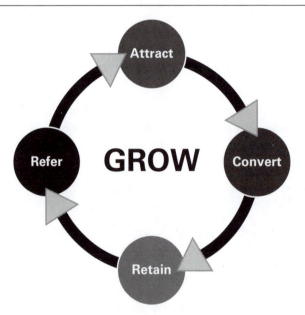

In the part on Pitch Big you only had how you looked as a business, and the preparation you'd done for the potential client, to make you attractive to them. The first sale is always the hardest; you've got limited or no proven history, so to the buyer you're a risk.

During the end-to-end sales process you manage to convert the prospect into a customer, having had a successful negotiation. You may have had to concede more than you would have liked, but the key fact is that you have a customer and can now prove that your business will live up to your promises.

Over time, and through consistent delivery, you retain the customer and as the relationship develops they become willing to give you a reference – and that's the point at which you've added the third-party endorsement to your process of attraction, and that's why I refer to it as an upward spiral.

It doesn't happen quickly, but if you imagine customers and potential customers as being at stages on the cycle, you can manage the relationship with them accordingly.

Figure 10.4 gives a few pointers as to what actions you might want to consider to move a customer/potential customer forward on the cycle.

FIGURE 10.4 Actions you can consider in order to move a customer/potential customer through the four-step cycle towards the referral stage

Position on the cycle	Actions to move the customer/ potential customer forward
Attracted: You have, at the minimum, secured the exploratory meeting – there is sufficient interest from the retailer in your proposition for them to want to spend time with you to hear more.	This was the process as described in Chapter 8 on selling. If you identify a potential customer who is somewhere in the pre-contract cycle but who has agreed an exploratory meeting, they are at the attracted stage. By focusing on the sales process, including rigorous follow-up, you will move them to conversion.
Converted: You have successfully completed the negotiation, the retailer has agreed to buy and you have agreed to supply.	This was the process described in Chapter 9 on negotiation. Having moved an attracted customer to the point where they have placed an order/contract with you, it is now imperative that you deliver on all your promises in order to earn their trust and loyalty to move them towards retained. You need to draw on all the preparation you did in Chapter 6 on scalability, to ensure that there are no operational failures and you will move them into retention.

FIGURE 10.4   *continued*

Position on the cycle	Actions to move the customer/ potential customer forward
Retained: You have secured a repeat order, or a further roll-out. Your customer has been satisfied with your service delivery and has increased the amount of business they have placed with you since the initial contract was signed.	This stage happens only as a result of your business operating effectively and consistently. You'll achieve this position with a customer only when there is additional spend or further extension to the original contact agreed. You need to encourage them to offer a reference for you, and to provide testimonials and case studies, as soon as is reasonable. Having prior agreements in place, as a result of a good negotiation phase, will make determining the right time to ask for this far easier as it will have been agreed, subject to your meeting defined success criteria. When you've achieved that point you can move forward to having a signed-off case study and becoming referenceable.
Referenced: You have received a signed-off case study that you can use in your PR and marketing.	You just need to keep them at this stage, and then you can call on them to support you at conferences/events or to provide a reference call to potential future customers. This referenceable position is where you ideally want to get all your customers to be. This is where they begin to contribute to your attraction stage and hence why this process is a cycle of growth.

Wrapping up

In this chapter we have discussed expansion from the perspective of growing your customer base. We have covered:

- ensuring you deliver on your customer promises and develop quality case studies;
- using those case studies to develop PR and marketing materials;
- how, through consistently delivering on your customer promises, you can create an upward spiral of growth.

In the next chapter we'll look at how you can deliver on your promises to the expanded customer base, getting big and staying big through replication.

11 Replication

Introduction

In this chapter we'll focus on how you can consistently and sustainably deliver on your customer promises by replicating your business. Replication is all about having the ability to repeat what you do well in order to do it more often, in greater volume, for more customers, to underpin your growth. It's about developing your robust, repeatable platform in order to become a scalable, saleable enterprise. It's about increasing your ability to perform effectively and efficiently, not only the core operational functions such as product development, sales and marketing, customer services and supply chain but also back-office functions such as HR, IT, Finance and Legal.

We will cover:

- what replication is and why it is important;
- what you need to have in place to create your robust and repeatable, replicable business model;
- your role in the business after having created a replicable, growing enterprise.

What is replication and why is it so important?

The verb 'to replicate' simply means to repeat or reproduce. In your business, replication is exactly that – repeating and reproducing what you do in order to do more of it. When planning out your approach to business replication you should take the opportunity to review what works in your business and what doesn't. It's about knowing what adds value and what is a waste of time. It's about stripping out the wasted effort and ensuring that you're focused on doing more of the good stuff. You don't necessarily want to repeat and reproduce everything you do; only the activities that support the delivery of your customer promises and that enable your business to be profitable.

So when I talk about replication I mean doing more of what you do well, cutting out waste and inefficiency, so that the business can maintain a consistent level of service and quality, meeting customer expectations, while at the same time sustaining profitable growth. It's all about first becoming a big small business, then a small big business, and finally a global mega-brand!

The reason we're focusing on replication now is that as a result of having just focused on expansion, attracting more customers, it's essential to ensure that you'll be able to support those customers. Right from the outset you must have in mind the need to develop processes and systems that can be repeated. Your business will never grow if every time you encounter an issue or a challenge you have to reinvent the wheel. You need to have a mentality such that every time you encounter something for the first time, you say to yourself 'how did we tackle that, what did we learn, what can we do better next time, what is the process that we can build from this experience to ensure it's easier/more efficient next time?'. With that sort of attitude in the early days you'll discover that when you hit the growth wave you're in a far stronger position to take advantage of it – the business won't come crashing down like a house of cards.

Replication is subtly different from scalability, which we covered in Chapter 6, in the part on Plan Big. Scalability is more about capacities, how much you can cope with, what your tipping points are in terms of output, lead times and quantities. Scalability is about knowing how much output you can produce/achieve with your current infrastructure. Replication is the next step – it's essentially saying 'knowing that with my current capacity I can output X and achieve profitability of Y, if I was to double my current capacity by investing in infrastructure, then, leveraging economies of scale, I should achieve a minimum output of 2X and profitability of greater than 2Y'. It's also about removing you, the business owner, from being a potential bottleneck.

If you want to grow your business you need to replicate your time, knowledge and activities either by systemizing things, by outsourcing things, or by training others to do the things you do. It can be tedious – no one will ever be able to do what you do, or as much as you do, in your business. Nor will they be able to do things to your standards or at your pace. You have to realize that, accept it, and proceed with an approach that is the best it can be. You have to appreciate that, as the owner, your knowledge, passion, determination and ambition will far exceed that of any employee. You have to develop your processes and systems to be 'foolproof' so that when followed the team around you can come close to delivering the same quality of output as you would have done. You have to accept that sometimes 80 per cent is good enough.

So really, when we think about replication at the formative stages of your business, it's all about taking steps. From starting up, the first step is to become a big small business, the next step is to become a small big business, and finally to become a global mega-brand.

Investors or future buyers will be looking for evidence of your ability to deliver sustained growth and proof that as a business owner you have not allowed yourself to become a bottleneck. This is a key decision factor that financiers will bear in mind before offering financial support to your business. If you decide to seek external funding to expand the business – perhaps to increase capacity, invest in infrastructure or to start up in new markets – your business will be scrutinized by the bank or any investors. They need to know that their investment is not at obvious risk (of course, any investment is a risk, but some risks are clearly much greater than others). One sanity check on this is that, to put it bluntly, you need to make sure that your business could continue to trade, to still produce profit, if you dropped dead tomorrow! Think about it – banks and investors are considering investing what might be a considerable amount of financial capital into your business; they will need to be sure that they've assessed all the risks and have made a measured decision. Business owners who are a bottleneck, and businesses that can't run independently of them, are a worry to investors and banks, and rightly so.

This is something close to my heart; I'd like to share a story with you about how my parents realized that in order to fulfil their retirement dream, to sell their manufacturing/retailing business for the best possible value, they needed to focus on replicating their skills and knowledge. I was a teenager at the time that this all took place and I think that this story also explains where I first started my personal 'love affair' with processes and systems!

CASE STUDY

My parents' business, Econermine Ltd, was created in the 1970s. Econermine retailed made-to-measure curtains and fine furnishings, predominantly by mail order, but also from a showroom attached to the factory and through concessions in other retail outlets. With a factory, a warehouse, a showroom and administrative offices all on one site, the business employed around 50 people. It was a significant local employer as, in rural Lincolnshire, beyond the Royal Air Force and farming, there was little other industry/employment.

The main route to consumers was through full-page advertising in the colour supplements that were included with Sunday newspapers. The business spent literally thousands of pounds each week on advertising. Consumers responded to the adverts by phone or by returning a coupon to request a full brochure. Brochures were sent out and customers would measure up, decide on their colour/style/fabric preferences, and then phone through with an order or complete a paper order form and post it back to the business. By the mid-1980s the business was doing quite well, although my parents worked all hours and essentially managed everything themselves.

In the mid-1980s two specific events made my parents decide to review the business model. The first was that the national home furnishings retail chain, Rosebys,* where Econermine had concessions, expressed an interest in acquiring the business.

My parents were open to the idea, recognizing that selling the business would enable them either to take early retirement or to get involved with other ventures that freed up their time from the long hours they currently were working. However, as Rosebys began to perform their due diligence as part of the acquisition process, investigating the inner workings of the business, they got cold feet and finally declared that the business was nothing without my parents; they said 'when we lose you we have very little'.

---

* Rosebys, like many other UK retailers, did not survive the downturn and entered administration in September 2008.

The second event that contributed to their determination to review the business was in response to media coverage about mail order businesses and 'off the page' sellers who sold direct to consumers through glossy magazines and Sunday supplements. A TV show had raised concerns as to the authenticity of mail order businesses, suggesting that some were bogus, fraudulently obtaining cash from consumers and never shipping the goods. The public became suspicious and this had a direct impact on Econermine's turnover.

As a result of these two events – the loss of an interested buyer and the shift in consumer confidence – my parents decided that the business needed to impress upon the consumer that they were a reputable brand, and to impress upon future buyers that they were a sustainable business, even without them at the helm. Their answer was to work to obtain the British Standards Institute 'Kitemark' as this would engender trust and ensure that a total quality management system was in place for the business.

Obtaining the BSI certification was a difficult process; until that point it had mainly been used to endorse engineering businesses, and Econermine was the first curtain maker to apply. It was also initially very difficult for staff to grasp the concept of having audited (robust and repeatable) processes and systems, a prerequisite of the BSI Kitemark being awarded.

However, what my parents discovered, as they ploughed through the process of documenting *all* processes and implementing state-of-the-art manufacturing and business information systems, was that having an audited process discipline was a great way to improve efficiency in every way.

The outcome of having completed the journey was, for example, the office team recording every customer complaint, no matter how trivial, and the quality team evaluating every customer return in detail. These customer failures (any customer not 100 per cent satisfied in a total quality management environment constitutes a failure) were reviewed each month and the most significant issues were addressed by refining the processes.

The office manager and operations manager began to really embrace this approach of documenting processes, reporting on issues, analysing root causes and improving processes for the future. Thus, through their example, it became the culture for the entire business.

The new processes and systems, failure elimination and higher customer service levels had a significant and positive impact on profitability. Most important though was the impact on the value of the business to a potential buyer.

Having completed the process of implementing a total quality management approach, having achieved the award of BS5750 Kitemark, and having also traded through the 1990s recession, my parents proactively put the business up for sale. By the mid-1990s it was a wholly different proposition, almost unrecognizable when compared to the business that Rosebys had dismissed. It was now highly organized, very profitable and had a positive cash flow. Owing to robust and repeatable processes and systems my parents had also demonstrated how they could easily abstract themselves from the day-to-day running of the business. The investors and buyers were impressed by the Kitemark, and as a result of what had been required to achieve the Kitemark, they were extremely pleased with the findings when they performed their due diligence. The business looked like a profit-generating machine; the directors (my parents) could not be considered a bottleneck, and were now simply seen as the owners of that valuable machine.

The business was sold for a very healthy sum in the mid-1990s. My parents' ambition had been realized and the investment in processes and systems paid off enormously. They had built a scalable, *saleable* enterprise based on the foundations of robust and repeatable processes and systems.

I hope this story illustrates the importance of replication as a fundamental enabler of both profitable growth and business value. The next question, of course, is how to go about it...

Developing your robust and repeatable platform

Developing your robust and repeatable platform mainly comes down to mentality and approach. If you always have the future in mind, then, whenever you encounter something new or unusual in the day-to-day running of the business, you can weigh up if there needs to be a defined approach to deal with that occurrence in the future. You need to be thinking about how your business can leverage people, processes and systems in order to reproduce what it does now in the most efficient way for the future.

You need to begin to create an operating manual, documenting the processes and policies that define the way of working for every area of your business. You don't have to do it all yourself – it could be a good project for a graduate intern to tackle, but you will need at least to review and sign off the first pass of your new 'operating manual'.

You may think this is overkill for your small business, but if your sales and expansion efforts suddenly take off you'll be thinking 'thank goodness we prepared for this!' Some of the world's most well-known brands have achieved their incredible successes as a direct result of having invested effort in creating a robust, replicable business model. One of my sources of inspiration, perhaps another reason why I have such a passion for processes and systems, is McDonald's. Whether you love or hate their offer, you can't help but admire what they've achieved as a business. Their relentless focus on efficiency, consistency, service standards and quality standards have resulted in a customer experience that barely varies from store to store, in fact from continent to continent! The McDonald's approach to standardization of service delivery has been replicated by other chains and now we see brands such as Starbucks and Subway enjoying a similar level of global expansion. The offer is different; the principles that underpinned their growth and success are the same. Develop and refine an operating manual, then stick to it for as long as it's a profitable and appropriate way to deliver on your mission.

So, to be as successful as these companies you need to take a leaf out of their book and develop your own 'operating manual'. One of the easiest ways to document your business processes is with a simple flow chart – it's visual, clear, and steps the reader through each action they need to take or each decision they need to make. A process map can include screen shots of any systems you use, if that's a part of the process, making it clear and unambiguous. Process maps can include decision/check points and highlight which occurrences need to be escalated to management in order to be approved or addressed. It may sound like an overwhelming task, but step by step you can begin to tackle the creation of your business's operating manual. It'll be worth its weight in gold in the longer term – it'll provide the basis of a training guide for all new starters and a reference manual for processes that are done on an infrequent basis and are not part of day-to-day routines or habits.

Of course, not everything has to be done internally; there are some areas where you can outsource aspects of the business. As long as you're passing these over to a reputable, quality provider, who delivers a professional service and who will commit to a service level agreement, you may want to consider that as an alternative. Certainly in the early days outsourcing could be ideal for your growing business, until such time as the costs of insourcing are likely to be less than the costs of outsourcing.

What areas of business do you need to replicate?

It's important to consider all of the core areas of your business and plan for the future. It's about combining strategy with organizational design, so you may find that getting some external support on this would help you.

In terms of core areas of business, as a minimum I would expect you to include:

- **Marketing/PR/Communications**: These are the areas which present your brand to the outside world – so this would be everything from website copy to blogs to social media as well as structured advertising, brochures, e-mail campaigns and press copy. This part of the business is all about attracting potential customers.

- **Sales**: This is the area of business responsible for identification of targets, approaching targets, and for managing the pre-sales, the sale and the negotiation to contracting. Sales might then manage the customer relationship, with a team of people (the customer services function) working alongside them, or they may well hand that over after they have converted a potential customer into a customer.

- **Customer services**: This is the area of the business responsible for managing and maintaining the relationship with a customer from the moment the sale has been approved. It is a first point of contact for any enquiries, issues or complaints; the people who are fundamental to retaining your customers.

- **Supply chain and logistics**: These are the areas which support the delivery of your product or service – the actual physical infrastructure that enables you to keep your promises to your customers, providing what you sell in a timely manner and in line with your customer service level agreements. In this context I consider 'supply chain' as not only physical goods but all the 'actors' in the process of delivering on your customer promise, whether you are a product or services supplier. It's the ability of your supply chain to deliver on your promises, coupled with your customer services team, that helps your business to retain customers, giving them the confidence to refer you in future and to provide you with the kind of success stories that we talked about in the previous chapter, which your marketing, PR and communications people would use to attract more customers.

- **Business/Product development:** This is the area of the business which is responsible for continually evaluating the offer compared to the competition and the needs/wants of the customer base in order to evolve the offering to ensure it is relevant, appropriate and fit for purpose. This area may also be responsible for exploring opportunities to diversify into other areas, or new markets, to add additional revenue potential to the business.

- **HR:** This area supports the planning of the whole organizational structure – the roles and responsibilities, what skills and knowledge are required. They also provide support in recruitment and training. The key value of an HR function is the provision of employment contracts and policies that ensure you are functioning ethically and legally, abreast of complex employment law and are able to take action to address any unsuitable employee behaviours.

- **Legal:** This is a very specialist area, so probably outsourced, although often managed by your internal finance team. It is possible that more than one legal practice may be appointed to support the wide range of commercial needs of the business, simply because legal practices tend to have strong specialisms and not all offer the full range of services that a business might require. A legal 'function' would support you in ensuring that you were compliant with regard to any regulatory considerations and protected in any complex contractual commitments (eg leasehold or capital procurement contracts). In addition, they can help you to protect your brand and intellectual property rights – critical for a supplier of products or services.

- **Finance**: This area not only manages your book-keeping, suppliers/customers invoicing, cash flow and banking, tax and payroll but would also include annual accounting, management reports, risk management, internal audit and statutory compliance. A good finance team (in-house or outsourced) can help you optimize your income, stay on the right side of all the legislation for company reporting and taxation, and also provide a commercial 'conscience' to the business when it comes to decision making.

- **IT**: This is a part of modern business that we can't live without! IT is responsible for delivering relevant, appropriate business information tools, transactional, back-office and reporting systems, all of which enable you to have access to data and information so that you can manage your business effectively.

What you need to be doing is appraising your core business areas in terms of what you do now (who is responsible for the area, how it is delivered) and what you need to be doing in future to provide a robust, replicable platform for that business area. Then you need to be assessing:

- what needs to be implemented to go from where you are now to where you want to be;

- when you ideally want to have achieved it by;

- if any investment is required (eg more resources, better computer systems etc).

You should complete the grid in Figure 11.1 to bring this to life – in the first row I've added examples of the sort of questions you should be asking yourself in order to complete it effectively. It will be very different for each and every business, not least as you'll probably have strong views about what can and cannot be outsourced, what should or should not be done by employees versus contractors etc. If you prefer not to make notes directly in the book, this template can be downloaded from the resources area via **www.retailchampion.co.uk/ selling-to-retailers/resources**.

FIGURE 11.1 Appraising your core business functions and determining what your requirements are for the future

Business area	Current position	Planned future position	Actions required to get there	Any costs?
Marketing/PR/ Communications	Consider what you have in place, who does this now, if it is done at all. Be honest with yourself.	What do you ideally want? Do you favour in-house or outsourced? What kind of expectations do you have of this area of your business?	Look at the difference between what you want and what you have. Plan out how you can get to where you want to be. What, if any, interim steps should you have along the way?	Try to estimate the overall cost to not only complete the actions that get you from where you are to where you need to be, but also consider what ongoing budget, approximately, you should allocate to this function. Try to do this in the context of not only the amount of resource required but with a sense-check as to the value-add to the business overall that this resource/functional area brings.
Sales				
Customer services				

Supply chain and logistics	Business/ Product development	HR	Legal	Finance	IT

Once you've completed the grid you'll have a fair idea as to where you're overstretched in some areas, undersupported, and where you need to invest to take the business forward. You'll also quickly see *who* is being overstretched – it's probably you, the business owner. You'll see just how overstretched you are and be more able to identify which areas should be top priority for delegation to others to help free up some of your time, remove you from being a bottleneck, and enable the business to move away from being constrained by time and resources and towards the ultimate aim of being a fully replicable, unconstrained operation.

Of course, as your business grows and as you delegate more and more of what you're doing to others, you may begin to reflect on your place within the business: your role, your purpose and your future.

I've had some heart-to-heart conversations with business owners in the past, and for their confidentiality I'm not going to share specific examples, but I would say it's a natural evolution for you, as your business grows, to think about your business as 'your baby'. Your business is something you've conceived and grown, and as it becomes able to operate independently of you, you may begin to feel quite emotional about it – the way parents feel when they see their children blossoming into capable adults – a mixture of pride, anticipation and a sadness that there is no going back. I've seen tough, commercially astute, grown men shed a tear over moving up and moving on with the businesses they created, so don't think that this sort of emotion is only for the 'romantics'. What is true is that it's a whole lot easier to face the inevitable changes that will happen if you've thought about them in the early days and planned ahead. That's what we'll look at in the last part of this chapter.

Your role in the business you've created

When you started your business, in fact before you started, you might have had a dream about what it would become. Many people seem to forget that they make a journey with their business, and if their business becomes *big* they need to be ready to deal with the impact that this has on them as the founder.

There are obviously both positive and negative aspects of being the owner of a business. On the plus side you are master of your own destiny, the choices you make you have to stand by, reaping the rewards or suffering the consequences. For most who go into business it's this liberation from the mechanics of employment, this sense of 'I am creating something, this is all down to me' that exhilarates them and drives them forward. On the downside it's incredibly hard work, you always get paid last (after suppliers, employees and the tax man have had their share) and when everyone else can go home and switch off (it's just a job) you can't. It's 24/7. You are quite literally like a parent when you own a business, because it's not just a job for you, and chances are you've invested your passion, dreams and financial security into it. Like parents do with their kids!

When your business grows into what you dreamed it would become, you can't just sit back and say 'what's next' – it's a living entity and you are still responsible for it. You need to make sure that it is in good hands if you no longer want to be involved, for instance.

There are many things you might want to consider, right from the outset, in terms of what you want for *you* when you have reached your initial goal within your business:

1 Will you reset new goals, and keep going? Is it still as exciting for you as it was in the beginning and are you still as passionate and motivated as you were?

2 Will you want to be a managing director/CEO or chairman of a big company? Would you be comfortable delegating and letting others just get on with it? Would *big* business and the associated complexities and politics bore you?

3 Will you want to sell the business and start something new? Is it the creation of a new business, bringing a new idea to life and watching it flourish, that inspires you and motivates you? Would you rather pass it on and simply be known as the founder so you can be free to do other things?

4 Or is your plan to sell and retire? Is this period of focus and hard work about achieving a step en route to some other plans for your life that creating a business and selling it will make possible for you?

There could be so many more questions to add. You need to be thinking about these and other questions when you're creating your business. If you plan ahead then when you do reach the point that you've expanded, replicated and grown, and you're no longer getting the same buzz that perhaps you once did, it won't come as a shock to you because you'd prepared for that right from the start.

Wrapping up

In this chapter we have discussed the importance of replication from the perspective of developing a robust, repeatable platform from which you can get big and stay big.

We have discussed:

- what replication is;
- developing your replicable business model;
- what your role in, or out, of the business might be in future.

In the final chapter we'll talk about why you need to ensure you retain a healthy dose of paranoia in your business if you don't just want to get big but also want to stay big...

Paranoia!

Introduction

In this, the final part of the 12-point plan, I'm going to talk about why it's a good thing to retain a reasonable amount of paranoia within the business! I am sure you're eager to get started on your action plan by now, so this will be a relatively brief chapter.

To get big and stay big, all of the parts of the 12-point plan are relevant; it's not a one-time review, but something that really requires continuous re-evaluation so that you keep in tune with the details. To become, and to remain, a big business you should ensure that you are always as focused on your goals and as hungry for success as you were when you first started out, and you need to breed that ethos throughout your business so that everyone has the same drive and passion.

So, in this final chapter we're going to:

- validate what I mean when I say 'paranoia';
- revisit the importance of being aware of the threat of new entrants;
- reflect on how you can keep pace with the ever-changing demands of the customer (in this case your end user, be that the consumer if you are a product supplier, or a function within the retail business if you are a services supplier);
- discuss how you should develop a continuous improvement culture, right from the outset, as a strategy to avoid becoming complacent.

Why a healthy dose of 'paranoia' is important

I hope you realize that when I use the term 'paranoia' I am being slightly 'tongue in cheek'. You should always feel slightly nervous about the competition, slightly worried about the customer going elsewhere, and concerned that the processes could be better. It's about channelling this 'nervous energy' that you feel in order to deliver a very positive outcome for your business. It's about avoiding complacency. There are negative connotations of the word paranoia – that's not what this is about!

The most successful businesses don't ever rest on their laurels; they are constantly paranoid that they will lose market share to new entrants or that their customers will become disillusioned with their products/services. They invest a great deal in retaining their position, knowing their competition and reinventing their offer to ensure they remain relevant to their customer. If you want a successful business you too must avoid complacency and ensure that you build a healthy dose of paranoia into your business culture. Imagine your business constantly checking over its shoulder, to see who's hot on its heels – that's the kind of 'paranoia' I am talking about!

Being aware of the threat of new entrants

After all the hard work you've done, you don't want to let those start-up up-starts steal your hard-earned market share! Right from the outset you need your business culture to reflect your desire always to remain ahead of the competition.

To do that you need to know who the competition are – and this is a constantly changing situation. Go back to Chapter 1 on identity and check which businesses belong in your competitive set, then go back to Chapter 5 on competition, and analyse them in greater detail. In the main, you'll find that the biggest changes to your competitive analysis will come from the 'new entrants' – these are businesses that, like you, want to have a slice of the market in which you will now have become established. Like you, they are probably very determined, hungry for success, efficient, agile and passionate. Unlike you, they have no past track record, no established ways of working, and thus face all the same barriers you faced at the beginning. And yet you got big. And they will too, if you let them. Suddenly your place in the Porter's Five Forces analysis has shifted; you need to imagine how, when you are an established business, you will fend off the threat of new entrants. When we reviewed it in Chapter 5 it was more from the perspective of *you* being the new entrant. When you are a big player, you're looking at the same situation from a very different perspective.

My advice is simple really. When you are expanding and replicating you need to retain those processes, behaviours, traits and 'personality' of your business that captured the very essence of what it was all about in the early days. Try to create a culture where every customer is as important and as valuable to you as the first, for instance. Be humble – make yourself, as the owner, accessible to clients, not in a protected ivory tower. Think of all the endearing, winning features of your small business and try to retain those when you get big. It's impossible ever to return to the 'seat of your pants' existence of being that small, new, developing business but at least you can ensure that you build accessibility, responsiveness, customer-centricity and flexibility into your growth strategy.

There will be new start-ups, and some of them will encroach on your market share, but if you build the business from the beginning with time dedicated to getting ahead and staying ahead, this will be much more a part of the culture of the business. It's better to be aware of the evolution in your marketplace, and to adapt to survive, than one day to wake up to discover your big business is under attack from a whole host of new entrants that you didn't see coming.

The other group you need to keep a relentless focus on is your customers. We'll discuss that next.

Don't assume you know your customer – keep checking!

It's not just the competition that will be constantly evolving, your customers will too. You need to be mindful of this and keep track of all the factors that influence them, be that the consumer if you are a product supplier, or a function within the retail business if you are a services supplier. You must ensure that you can evolve your offering in line with their needs and wants, future-proofing your business against the inevitable developments in technology and trends that affect what your customers want and how they behave.

You need to reflect on how you can develop, from the outset, processes that ensure your business keeps pace with the ever-changing demands of your customer: plan regular reviews, research and monitoring to ensure that your proposition does not drift away from what customers want (and that your customers don't drift away from your proposition). Reflect back on Chapter 4 on the customer: what can you be doing to maintain relevance and to keep in touch with their needs and wants? In Chapter 11 on replication, I highlighted the potential need for a business/product development function. Typically this area of your business would be responsible for looking forward, tabling new ideas, producing innovation, and developing solutions to problems that customers didn't even know they had yet. This function's purpose is to keep the offer evolving and relevant for the long term.

The successes of Diva Cosmetics and Magic Whiteboard were down to Emma's and Neil's deep knowledge and insight into their end user. Emma invested heavily in really understanding the customer base of each retailer she approached, and never assumed that this stayed the same. For each new range or product idea presented to a retailer she re-evaluated the customer base. As she offered a fashion item she needed to ensure she was absolutely on-trend and aligned to the very rapidly changing needs and wants of each of her customers' customer groups.

Neil had been the end user of the original concept for his brand, but as he expanded into retail he recognized that an office user had a wider range of requirements. His team developed an extended range of products to provide those office users with a greater choice and to serve their customers' customer better. They diversified into various products, including Magic 'sticky notes' and a Magic Blackboard too!

All successful businesses evolve their offer to remain relevant, to grow and to become more 'valued' by their customer. You should too. You should maintain a relentless focus on your customer needs and have an in-built concern that they *will* leave you if you don't keep the focus on them. Once again, a healthy dose of paranoia will ensure that you don't get complacent and that you always strive to add value to your customer base.

Developing a continuous improvement culture

Remember the robust and repeatable processes you developed in the last chapter? Well, you don't just document them once and then leave them to gather dust in a filing cabinet or saved electronically and then ignored for years. If you want to stay big then, along with constant review of the competition and customer, you need also to review your ways of working, to learn from experiences and enhance your processes to be more relevant to delivering the offer and more focused on efficiency. It fits well into a chapter on paranoia because continuous improvement reflects a mentality of always believing that things can be improved – a healthy dose of paranoia keeps you feeling that things aren't quite good enough yet!

This is the basis of a continuous improvement culture; it means that right from the outset you, your team, and all those around you feel empowered to ask questions about why things are the way they are and to see if perhaps they could be better. Having a culture that encourages all those in the business to question the status quo can be challenging to manage, but it does mean that you'll be picking up on suggestions, innovation and ideas from a range of people. Among the inevitable 'noise' there may well be some ideas so brilliant that you can't wait to get on and implement them! It's a balancing act to get the culture right – you want people to follow the processes in order to deliver a consistent level of service, to have a replicable business model etc. You also want them to feel able to question those very processes if they genuinely believe they could be better, more efficient, easier, quicker, lower cost, higher quality etc. It's down to your leadership, and later the leadership of your management team, to create the environment for providing improvement suggestions without creating a situation where nothing is done and everyone is questioning.

If you focus on always designing processes that are going to have longevity, preparing you for the potential future needs of the business, it may feel like you are developing something beyond what you need right now. That's fine, you are, but you'll need it in future and if at that point you've got teams who are familiar with best practice then you'll have less to worry about. I'll give you an example.

CASE STUDY

A small business I worked with wanted to have a CRM system. This would enable them to identify their ideal target customers, track progress and share information about the status of each potential customer/customer engagement with their team of sales people and customer services staff. They initially designed the process and developed simple tracking using a spreadsheet. This evolved and developed as they used it. Both the processes (the way of using the data in the spreadsheet) and the tool (the spreadsheet itself) were adapted over time to best support what the team needed in order to do their job efficiently and successfully. After a period of time they had a stable and established process; the team using the tools understood how they needed to interact with the spreadsheet in order to share information about their progress with a particular potential customer or the status of an existing customer.

The business owner was planning just to upgrade the spreadsheet to a simple in-house database; it would make it more robust, and it would 'do for now'. However, and with some coaching, that owner realized that for a minimal additional cost (compared to creating the in-house database) he could actually purchase a high-quality software solution to support the CRM process. It also had additional benefits of functionality he didn't yet need. With encouragement he did go for the software solution, and it was a good decision. That extra functionality supported a customer call centre, something he didn't have at the time. Within a year he needed to explore setting up a customer call centre, and by having chosen a system that was more 'state of the art' he had essentially also ensured the longevity of its relevance to the business processes. This, of course, meant that the small additional cost was paid back very rapidly because the system was suitable for the business for the longer term and supported their growth with limited change and no further investment required.

My advice is always to go for something that's more comprehensive, more robust than you need now (as long as it is affordable) because it will usually pay back over its lifetime and will mean less need for regular change and the associated disruption to the business.

Finally, if you really want to focus on continuous improvement, I'd suggest that you make a point of running through all of the prior 11 points of the 12-point plan on an annual or bi-annual basis. This will help you to validate, sense-check or confirm that your entire business proposition and approach are still relevant, congruent and appropriate for your customer. Each time you revisit each part you may find that there are a couple of actions you'd like to add to your checklist, to take you forward from where you are now to where you want to be. Essentially that's continuous improvement. As long as you never rest on your laurels or get complacent, and maintain a healthy dose of paranoia in your business, you'll get big and stay big.

Wrapping up

In this chapter it's been all about retaining a healthy dose of paranoia, not getting complacent, and being sure that no matter how big your business grows you embed the processes of re-evaluation of your proposition. We've talked about how that re-evaluation should ensure that you know the competition, know the new entrants, stay relevant with the offering, keep reinventing yourself and always strive to achieve with the same ambition as when you started out.

We have discussed:

● being aware of new entrants;

● focusing on the ever-changing demands of the customer;

● developing a continuous improvement culture.

Before we move on to the conclusion, where we'll briefly discuss your action plan, we'll wrap up this fourth and final part – 'Get Big, Stay Big!'.

In this final part we have been focusing on creating a growth wave for your business and making sure that all of your operations and core business functions are prepared to keep the momentum going.

Having completed the three chapters on expansion, replication and paranoia, we have covered how to:

1   leverage success stories from your existing customer base to develop marketing and PR that will attract new customers;

2   develop a robust and repeatable platform for growth;

3   avoid complacency setting in.

As in the prior parts, we'll wrap up this part on 'Get Big, Stay Big!' with a simple checklist (Figure 12.1) for you to go through to make sure that you're clear about what the ingredients are to implement an effective and sustainable growth strategy. As always, this is available for download via **www.retailchampion.co.uk/selling-to-retailers/resources**.

continued on page 229

FIGURE 12.1 Part Four checklist

Area	Ingredient	Complete? (yes/no)	Action to address (if any)	Cost implications?	Priority (H/M/L)	Target date to complete
Expansion	Ensuring you deliver on your customer promises and develop quality case studies					
Expansion	Incorporating case studies into PR and marketing					
Expansion	Creating an upward spiral of growth through consistently delivering on your customer promises					
Replication	Understanding what replication is and why it is important					
Replication	Planning how you can develop and implement your robust and repeatable, replicable business model					

FIGURE 12.1 *Continued*

Area	Ingredient	Complete? (yes/no)	Action to address (if any)	Cost implications?	Priority (H/M/L)	Target date to complete
Replication	Considering your role in the business after having created a replicable, growing enterprise					
Paranoia	Staying aware of the competition and particularly looking out for new entrants					
Paranoia	Maintaining focus on the ever-changing demands of the customer (in this case your end user, be that the consumer or a function within a retail business)					
Paranoia	Developing a continuous improvement culture, not becoming complacent					

Part Four: Get Big, Stay Big! – summing up *continued*

With this, and all the other parts that have gone before, your business should be well prepared to become a scalable, saleable enterprise through selling to retailers.

Conclusion

The very final part of the journey is to discuss your action plan. It's one thing to have walked through the 12-point plan, but quite another to ensure that you keep going and keep working towards your goal.

Having completed all four parts you should now have four end-of-part checklists with actions, costs, priorities and due dates. This is great, but only if you actually then implement those actions. My advice is that if you're the sort of person who will create the plan, then ignore it, getting on with the day job, you should seek the advice of a business mentor or coach. Externalizing the plan, sharing it with an independent third party, will not only put more pressure on you to make sure you deliver it, but the third party can also act as a conscience to you, checking up on you to make sure you make progress. If you struggle with any areas, a good coach/mentor will be able to guide you or help you recognize when you need the support of an expert third party on the topic.

Of course, if you are a proactive person who doesn't need anyone chasing up then that's great, you'll be able to get on with it right away.

I want to write only a single page by way of conclusion, so to wrap up I'd like to thank you for reading this book, for completing the journey with me. I hope you now feel fired up, armed with everything you need to do to sell successfully to retailers. Don't forget to visit the resources area to download some of the items shared in this book – **www.retailchampion.co.uk/selling-to-retailers/resources** – you can request your access pin using the code on page xvi.

All that remains is to wish you the very best of success with your venture.

Clare Rayner,
The Retail Champion

APPENDIX 1
The Retail Champion

The Retail Champion – mission

The Retail Champion offers **retail expertise and bespoke business mentoring programmes** to business owners who are either retailers or suppliers to retail. With The Retail Champion businesses will **develop robust and repeatable processes and systems,** underpinning their future growth and success. The Retail Champion programmes help businesses to **become scalable, saleable enterprises.**

How The Retail Champion can help you!

The Retail Champion mentoring programmes can be tailored to provide you with mentoring, advice, support, consultancy, project management and training. Clients comment that the advice, support, guidance and expertise delivered by The Retail Champion have been invaluable to their businesses.

Typically clients are small, independent retailers or suppliers to retail. The reasons clients give for choosing to work with The Retail Champion are lack of time, lack of retail expertise, or lack of confidence in making tough decisions to really drive their businesses forward on their own... The Retail Champion fills the gaps by:

- keeping you on track, **focusing your time** on the value-added activities that achieve your business aims and objectives;
- **sharing expertise** and helping you to develop strategies to increase profit, customer base, revenue streams and channels to market;

- acting as a sounding board for your ideas, providing feedback and validation from an expert third party to **give you the confidence that you are making the right choices!**

1-2-1 mentoring programmes with The Retail Champion are offered to a maximum of 10, non-competing businesses at any point in time. These businesses benefit from working hand in hand with Clare Rayner. Your programme is uniquely tailored to your needs and includes regular contact (face to face, e-mail, phone, webinar) so that your business can benefit from working with one of the UKs most well-known retail experts without breaking the bank!

www.retailchampion.co.uk

APPENDIX 2
Independent Retailer Month UK

Independent Retailer Month is a global 'shop local' campaign that runs throughout July. The campaign highlights the important role that small, independent retailers play in the communities they serve, the local economy they contribute to, and in the retail sector as a whole.

Created in the United States, Independent Retailer Month UK, which launched in July 2011, is led by Clare Rayner, The Retail Champion.

The initiative aims to:

- impact the independent retail sector globally with relevant support, expertise and insights;
- connect consumers and communities with local retailers, reminding them of the benefits of shopping local;
- engage small business organizations, networks and thought-leaders to promote the importance of independent retail to the global, national and local economies.

Retailers and suppliers to retail are encouraged to get involved. Retailers should focus on working together with their neighbouring retailers to provide activities, promotions and events throughout July that will engage their local community, increasing footfall, sales and loyalty. Suppliers to retail should work with retailers to offer them support for their promotions, activities and events, recognizing that smaller, independent retailers are a valuable route to market for those who supply product and a valuable source of income for those who supply services.

www.independentretailermonth.co.uk

APPENDIX 3
The Retail Conference

The Retail Conference – mission

The Retail Conference is the UK's leading retail industry forum for senior decision makers and those who define business strategy in the retail sector to meet, network and share their success stories. Delivered by retailers, for retailers, hosted in a quality venue with exceptional catering and facilities, this is a not to be missed event. All attendees should expect a very worthwhile and informative day away from the office.

About The Retail Conference

The Retail Conference, which is organized by Retail Acumen, was first delivered in 2007 and fast became the UK's leading conference for senior decision makers and those who define business strategy in the retail sector. The format encompasses keynote seminars, breakout sessions and workshops, a panel discussion and plenty of networking time.

The content is focused on real-life case studies, industry insights, examples of best practice in action, and thought-leadership. The event provides an engaging and inspiring learning experience for all those who attend. Uniquely, the content is focused on what really matters to retailers; topical, relevant and forward-looking.

The Retail Conference is different from other events for three key reasons:

1 It was the first true conference format event to offer *free* attendance to retailers.

2 All keynote speakers are guaranteed to be either experienced retail practitioners or representatives of best-practice

organizations. Sponsors only ever take to the stage when supporting their retail client.

3 Being a content-centric event, there is only ever one sponsor presenting on their core expertise. Sponsors are selected for their quality, credibility, proven track record and innovative concepts. Retailers can have confidence that if they want to take their conversations with the sponsors further, they are speaking to genuine industry experts.

When delegates attend The Retail Conference they benefit from:

- hearing from engaging speakers who are experts in a highly topical field;
- expanding their knowledge through workshops and breakout sessions;
- debating current issues with expert panellists in the panel discussion;
- gaining an insight into what other retailers are doing and seeing best practice in action;
- networking time with other retailers, sharing experiences, issues and challenges;
- taking time out to focus on what really matters in their business;
- renewed passion and enthusiasm and some great new ideas to put into practice!

www.retailconference.co.uk

APPENDIX 4
Retail Acumen

Retail Acumen – mission

Retail Acumen delivers deep, detailed analysis and insights into business performance for retail multiples. The specialist team leverage their love of detailed data analytics, combined with a deep understanding of the retail sector, to uncover practical, easily implementable, optimization opportunities. Clients benefit from recommendations that identify how simple business change can achieve maximum performance improvement, fast.

Retail Acumen – services

No professional can be expected to take a business decision with confidence without evidence to back it up. At Retail Acumen, it is our job to arm decision makers with the information they need to proceed confidently and significantly improve business performance in four key areas:

- increasing sales;
- intensifying assortment;
- improving return on space;
- optimizing supply chain.

www.retailacumen.com

e-mphasis Internet Marketing

e-mphasis Internet Marketing – mission

e-mphasis Internet Marketing is the supplier of choice for the delivery of local search marketing, e-commerce search marketing and mobile search marketing for businesses that serve the consumer (retail, hospitality and leisure.) e-mphasis's expert and innovative team consistently deliver exceptional, measureable and repeatable results so clients benefit from incremental sales and impressive ROI.

About e-mphasis Internet Marketing

e-mphasis Internet Marketing is a digital marketing agency that specializes in providing a range of search marketing services to clients whose customers are consumers – specifically those in retail, hospitality and leisure.

e-mphasis was founded by Andrew Rayner, a search marketing expert, who has been working with internet-related technologies since the internet came into existence. Andrew and the team at e-mphasis have developed innovative search marketing techniques to enable clients to get found online for their desired search terms. This increases the volume of relevant search traffic, which in turn has led to clients reporting uplifted sales that represent up to 30 times return on investment within just one year of engaging e-mphasis services!

e-mphasis offers search engine optimization, e-commerce search marketing, and has developed a unique local internet marketing service which is particularly effective for mobile search and event-based marketing. As a result of its focus on local search, e-mphasis is now considered to be the leading local search marketing expert in the UK.

www.e-mphasis.com

INDEX

NB: page numbers in *italic* indicate figures or tables